Beyond the Algorithm

Sovereignty, National Advancement and the Future of AI

Vinit Mojes
Vijaya Shankar Ganesan

Published By: Buddha International Publications

Website: https://www.buddhapublications.com/

E-mail: info@buddhapublications.com

Mobile: +91- 7011267635

Place: Delhi, Mumbai, Ludhiana, USA.

First Edition: 2025

MRP: 299/-INR

ISBN: 978-93-6884-052-7

[Printed In Delhi, Mumbai, Ludhiana, USA]

"In the beginning, man created AI in his own image. And then he spent years trying to teach it not to spam him with Instagram reels."

In the pages to come, we'll explore the art of wielding AI with wisdom, humor, and, ideally, a measure of restraint— always mindful that for all its algorithms, no machine will quite capture our blend of brilliance and absurdity."

Content

"The Philosophy of Sovereign AI: A Qualitative Insights Towards Prosperity"

1. Introduction

Imagine a world where haptic suits let you feel the virtual embrace of a long-distance friend, where digital coins jingle in your pocket as you conquer quests, and where the lines between humans and intelligent machines blur into a tapestry of ones and zeros. Welcome to the not-so-distant future depicted in Ready Player One, a cinematic rollercoaster that gives us a sneak peek into the transformative impact of artificial intelligence (AI) on our daily lives. While we may not all be donning VR headsets to escape into the OASIS just yet, AI is undeniably reshaping our reality—minus the epic car chases (for now).

From chatbots that help you order pizza (and occasionally misunderstand "pepperoni" as "extra anchovies") to algorithms predicting your next favorite song before you've even heard it, AI has woven itself into the fabric of modern society. But beyond these conveniences lies a weightier consideration: how do nations maintain control and autonomy—what we call ***Sovereign AI****—in a world where data streams cross borders more effortlessly than a viral dance challenge?*

Historically, sovereignty was about clear-cut borders and the right to defend them, as thinkers like Jean Bodin philosophized back when the most advanced technology was, well, the printing press. Fast forward to today, and the digital revolution is challenging these age-old notions faster than you can say "quantum computing." Data doesn't need a passport, and AI algorithms influence global markets while we're still debating daylight saving time.

Economically, AI is the new gold rush (minus the pickaxes), driving innovation, boosting productivity, and spawning industries we hadn't even dreamed of—professional esports commentator, anyone? Politically, AI aids governance through data-driven policymaking and public services that might know what you need before you fill out a 20-page form. Militarily, AI brings us into the realm of autonomous systems and cyber warfare, necessitating a fresh look at defense strategies—because nobody wants a rogue drone mistaking a picnic for a hostile takeover.

But let's not get too caught up in the shiny tech without pondering the profound questions it raises about our cultural identity, ethical norms, and human agency. As AI systems manage everything from delivering your mail (drones deftly dodging your neighbor's overenthusiastic sprinkler system) to diagnosing illnesses with a precision that makes WebMD look like a fortune cookie, society is undergoing a metamorphosis. This integration prompts us to reflect on employment (will robots take our jobs or just make them more interesting?), privacy (is your smart fridge judging your midnight ice cream habit?), and the future awaiting our children (will they ask, "What's a driver's license?").

Purpose and Scope

Embarking on this intellectual adventure, much like Wade Watts searching for Halliday's Easter egg, we aim to explore the philosophical underpinnings of **Sovereign AI** and its implications for national advancement. We'll dive into the annals of philosophical thought—minus the dusty tomes and plus a fresh pot of coffee—to understand how AI is redefining sovereignty and reshaping the human condition.

Our mission is twofold: first, to analyze the ethical, cultural, and societal dimensions of AI within the context of national sovereignty; second, to propose strategies for aligning AI development with human-centric values and philosophical principles (because let's face it, nobody wants to answer to an AI overlord with the empathy of a rock). We'll explore how education systems must adapt—hint: coding might become the new cursive—to prepare individuals for an AI-driven future. We'll also examine the tug-of-war between tech giants and individual innovators in steering AI's trajectory and consider the implications of AI in realms such as warfare (preferably avoiding any Terminator-esque scenarios), consciousness (can machines dream of electric sheep?), and cultural preservation (will AI appreciate Shakespeare or think he's just "old-school rap"?).

The roadmap for our exploration is as follows:

- **Section 1** explores the philosophical foundations of Sovereign AI, tracing historical concepts of sovereignty, ethical frameworks for AI, and human-centric philosophies—all presented in an accessible, thought-provoking manner.
- **Section 2** delves into the evolution of sovereignty in the digital age, examining how AI challenges traditional notions of state authority and regulation. It delves into ethical frameworks like utilitarianism, deontology, and virtue ethics to address AI's societal impact and advocates for human-centric development to balance technological advancement with cultural preservation and accountability.
- **Section 3** explores Japan's and India's approaches to implementing Sovereign AI, highlighting Japan's human-centric philosophy and technological advancements like Society 5.0 and space exploration.
- **Section 4** examines how AI can preserve cultural values, languages, and traditions while addressing its societal impact, including the role of humanoid robots in human interactions.
- **Section 5** examines the ethical and societal challenges of Sovereign AI, focusing on issues like bias, social equity, privacy, and surveillance. It explores philosophical debates on individual rights versus collective security and evaluates governance models, including top-down regulations and open-source movements.
- **Section 6** outlines strategies for aligning AI development with philosophical principles, emphasizing ethical frameworks, interdisciplinary collaboration, and education reform. It explores advancements in neuroscience and AI, the ethical implications of mind-uploading, and the need for international collaboration in AI governance while maintaining sovereignty. The section highlights blockchain as a tool for enhancing AI security and decentralization.
- **Section 7** delves into the evolving relationship between AI and humanity, exploring philosophical challenges like the singularity, transhumanism, and the essence of consciousness. It examines societal acceptance of AI robots, ethical frameworks for technological disruptions, and AI's role in space exploration.

  Through this exploration, we hope to contribute to the discourse on how nations can navigate the labyrinth of AI integration, ensuring that technological advancement harmonizes with ethical imperatives and promotes the prosperity of humanity—ideally without any Matrix-style glitches.

1.1 Contextualizing Sovereign AI

Defining Sovereign AI and its Relevance today

Sovereign AI refers to a nation's ability to develop, regulate, and deploy AI technologies independently, aligning them with its cultural values, ethical standards, and strategic interests. In a world where algorithms can influence everything from stock markets to social behavior—often without needing a passport—maintaining sovereignty over AI is akin to safeguarding a nation's future prosperity and security.

The relevance of Sovereign AI today cannot be overstated. As data becomes the new oil and AI systems integrate deeper into critical infrastructures, questions arise about who holds the reins of these powerful technologies. Dependence on foreign AI solutions may pose risks to national security, economic stability, and even cultural identity. It's not just about having robots that can deliver pizza (though that's a perk); it's about ensuring that the AI shaping our society reflects our collective values and priorities.

Tracing the Historical Evolution of AI

The journey of AI began in the mid-20th century, back when computers were the size of rooms and had less processing power than today's smartphones. In 1950, British mathematician Alan Turing posed the provocative question in his paper "Computing Machinery and Intelligence": "Can machines think?" This question wasn't just the spark for countless sci-fi plots; it laid the foundational challenge that would drive AI research for decades.

In 1956, the Dartmouth Conference marked the official birth of artificial intelligence as a field of study. Organized by visionaries like John McCarthy and Marvin Minsky, this gathering brought together brilliant minds eager to teach machines how to mimic human reasoning. McCarthy coined the term "artificial intelligence," ambitiously suggesting that "every aspect of learning or any other feature of intelligence can in principle be so precisely described that a machine can be made to simulate it." Talk about setting high expectations.

Marvin Minsky, often called the "father of AI," made significant contributions at MIT, focusing on cognitive simulation and the development of AI programs capable of problem-solving and pattern recognition. Their work laid the groundwork for the AI systems we see today, even if they couldn't have predicted we'd use their legacy to create chatbots that can debate pineapple on pizza.

The Transformative Impact of AI on National Development and Sovereignty

Fast forward to the 21st century, and AI has leaped from theoretical discussions into the heart of national development strategies. Economically, AI is driving innovation, boosting productivity, and creating entirely new industries. It's like discovering a gold mine but with algorithms instead of pickaxes.

- Reshaping Economies: AI technologies automate routine tasks, optimize supply chains, and enable data-driven decision-making. For example, financial institutions use AI to detect fraudulent transactions faster than a cheetah on espresso.
- Governance and Public Services: Governments employ AI for everything from predicting traffic patterns to optimizing energy consumption. Estonia, for instance, has embraced e-governance, using AI to provide public services efficiently—though we can't confirm if they've taught AI to handle the infamous DMV lines yet.

- National Security Enhancements: AI plays a pivotal role in cybersecurity, surveillance, and defense systems. Autonomous drones patrol borders, and AI algorithms analyze vast amounts of data to detect threats. It's like having a digital watchdog that never sleeps (and doesn't need tummy rubs).

Illustrations of AI in Everyday Life

- **Automated Postal Services:** Remember when mail delivery depended on human schedules and occasional canine interference? Today, AI-powered sorting machines process mail with remarkable speed and accuracy. Some countries are experimenting with delivery robots—though they sometimes get confused by squirrels.
- **Food Delivery Using AI and Robotics:** Craving sushi at 2 a.m.? AI algorithms coordinate delivery services to satisfy late-night cravings efficiently. Companies like Starship Technologies deploy autonomous robots to bring food right to your doorstep, navigating sidewalks better than some humans.
- **Automation of Mundane Tasks:** From robotic vacuum cleaners that keep your floors spotless (unless your pet sees them as mortal enemies) to smart home systems that adjust lighting and temperature based on your preferences, AI is freeing us from routine chores. This automation allows people to focus on more creative and fulfilling activities—like binge-watching the latest series without guilt.

Reflections on Jobs, Sustainability, and the Future of Our Children

While AI's contributions to efficiency and convenience are undeniable, they also prompt serious reflections on employment and societal structures. Automation threatens to displace workers in sectors like manufacturing, transportation, and even customer service. A report by the World Economic Forum suggests that while AI could displace 85 million jobs by 2025, it could also create 97 million new roles—though this transition might not be as smooth as upgrading your smartphone.

The sustainability of these changes hinges on our ability to adapt:

- **Education and Reskilling:** Preparing the workforce for an AI-driven economy requires a reimagining of education systems. Emphasizing STEM fields, critical thinking, and lifelong learning becomes essential. After all, coding might become as fundamental as reading and writing—though hopefully with fewer grammar rules.
- **Economic Policies:** Governments may need to consider policies like universal basic income or job guarantee programs to mitigate the impact of automation on employment. It's a delicate balance between embracing technological advancement and ensuring people aren't left asking, "Would you like fries with that AI?"
- **Future Generations:** For our children, the world of AI offers opportunities and challenges. They might grow up with AI tutors, personalized learning experiences, and careers we can't even imagine today. On the flip side, they'll face ethical dilemmas about privacy, digital footprints, and perhaps even robot rights—imagine debating whether your household AI deserves a day off.

1.2 Advanced AI and its Purpose

As we navigate this digital frontier, we find ourselves at the crossroads of technology and philosophy, much like Parzival deciphering the riddles in Ready Player One. While it's tempting to get swept away by the allure of AI's capabilities (who wouldn't want an AI assistant to handle laundry folding?), it's imperative to pause and ponder the deeper implications. This isn't merely about circuits and code; it's about the essence of humanity and the society we aspire to build.

Qualitative Insights and Philosophical Reflections

Examining AI through a philosophical lens is not just academic indulgence—it's a necessity. Philosophy equips us with the tools to critically analyze the ethical, cultural, and existential questions that AI inevitably raises. As Alan Turing famously asked, "Can machines think?" we must now ask, "Should machines think like us, and if so, how?" Understanding AI's impact requires more than technical expertise; it demands introspection about our values, responsibilities, and the kind of future we envision.

We need to delve into questions like:

- **Ethical Considerations:** How do we ensure AI operates within moral boundaries? Can we encode empathy and justice into algorithms, or will AI always reflect the biases of its creators (looking at you, biased facial recognition systems)?
- **Human Identity and Agency:** In a world where AI can compose symphonies, diagnose illnesses, and even debate philosophy (though perhaps not convincingly to Socrates), what does it mean to be human? How do we retain our agency when machines can outperform us in tasks, we once considered uniquely ours?
- **Cultural Impact:** Will AI lead to a homogenization of cultures, or can it be a tool for preserving and celebrating diversity? Imagine AI curating art that reflects indigenous traditions rather than just remixing Renaissance classics.

By focusing on these qualitative insights, we aim to move beyond the hype and fearmongering often associated with AI. Instead, we'll engage in a nuanced exploration that considers both the potentials and pitfalls, much like navigating the challenges of the OASIS without losing sight of the real world's value.

Objectives Of Having Advanced AI:

Our mission, should we choose to accept it (and we do), is guided by three core objectives:

1. **To explore how AI affects national advancement.**

We'll investigate how AI serves as a catalyst for economic growth, innovation, and enhanced public services. From smart cities that adjust traffic flow like a well-conducted orchestra to healthcare systems predicting epidemics faster than you can say "supercomputer," AI's role in national progress is profound.

Artificial Intelligence significantly contributes to national advancement by enhancing productivity and fostering innovation. A study by McKinsey Global Institute estimates that AI could add approximately $13 trillion to the global economy by 2030, increasing global GDP by about 1.2% annually.

- **Without AI Implementation:**

If a country's current GDP is $1 trillion with an annual growth rate of 2%:

GDP Year N=$1 trillion× (1+0.02) N

- **With AI Implementation:**

If AI boosts the growth rate to 3.2% (an additional 1.2%):

GDP Year N=$1 trillion× (1+0.032) N

After 10 Years:

- **Without AI:**

\$1 trillion× (1+0.02)10≈\$1.22 trillion

- **With AI:**

\$1 trillion× (1+0.032)10≈\$1.37 trillion

2. To assess the ethical, cultural, and societal implications.

This involves a candid look at the challenges AI poses. Will automation widen socioeconomic gaps or bridge them? How do we protect individual privacy when AI thrives on data (and lots of it)? Can we prevent a scenario where AI's "helpfulness" becomes an overbearing intrusion—think Clippy from Microsoft Word but with access to your entire life?

Average Cost of a Data Breach: \$3.86 million (IBM Security Report)

Probability of a Breach in Two Years: 29.6%

For 1,000 Companies:

- Expected Number of Breaches: 1,000 × 29.6% = 296 breaches
- Total Expected Cost: 296 × \$3.86 million ≈ **\$1.14 billion** (underscoring the societal cost and necessitates robust data protection strategies)

3. To propose strategies for aligning AI with human values.

Because an AI revolution without a moral compass could lead us down a dystopian path faster than you can say "Skynet." We'll offer recommendations for policy frameworks, ethical guidelines, and collaborative efforts to ensure AI development reflects our shared humanity.

Organizations can use key performance indicators (KPIs) to monitor adherence.

Mathematical Monitoring:

- **Transparency Index (TI):**

TI=Number of Explainable Decisions/Total Decisions×100%

- **Goal:** TI ≥ 95%

Example:

If an AI system made 10,000 decisions, and 9,800 are explainable:

TI=9,800/10,000×100%=**98**

The system meets the transparency goal, aligning with human values of trust and accountability. The mathematical models and calculations enable the quantification of abstract ethical principles making it possible to set measurable goals for AI systems.

Multi Agent Approach : Revolutionizing Education Using Personalized AI

Artificial intelligence (AI) revolutionizes education by enabling personalized, adaptive learning experiences. Traditional one-size-fits-all teaching models often fail to accommodate students' diverse learning speeds, styles, and needs. AI-powered tutoring systems address this challenge by offering scalable, customized instruction that adapts to the unique requirements of each learner. These intelligent tutors have the potential to bridge educational disparities, ensuring that both privileged and underprivileged students worldwide receive high-quality, customized learning experiences. The integration of cutting-edge AI techniques, including LoRA (Low-Rank Adaptation), QLoRA (Quantized LoRA), and multi-agent AI orchestration, enables unprecedented scalability and efficiency in education—bringing truly intelligent, real-time, and cost-effective tutoring to learners across the globe.

Background on AI in Education

Artificial Intelligence has seen rapid advancements in education, allowing automated tutoring, adaptive learning, and intelligent content delivery. AI-powered platforms analyze student behavior, learning patterns, and interaction data to optimize educational experiences. Moreover, modern AI-driven education systems leverage optimized model fine-tuning techniques such as LoRA and QLoRA to create intelligent tutors capable of running on consumer-grade GPUs with significantly reduced computational overhead. These advancements not only enhance efficiency and scalability but also make personalized learning more accessible than ever before.

The Need for Personalized AI in Learning

Every student has unique learning needs, yet traditional education systems follow a standardized approach that does not accommodate individual differences. Personalized AI-based tutoring adapts content and teaching strategies based on real-time student performance, engagement levels, and cognitive abilities. This is now made possible with QLoRA-based optimizations, enabling fine-tuned 7B+ parameter models to run efficiently on edge devices. By tailoring learning experiences, AI improves comprehension, retention, and student motivation while reducing the cost of deploying large-scale AI-driven education systems

Limitations of Traditional Educational Methods

Conventional educational systems are often constrained by the following:

- Lack of personalized instruction due to large class sizes.
- Static curricula that do not adapt to individual learning speeds.
- Limited teacher availability for one-on-one student interactions.
- Ineffective assessment methods that do not provide feedback.

To address these limitations, modern AI-powered, adaptive learning systems incorporate multi-agent architectures, real-time assessment engines, and AI-driven workflow orchestration using LangChain, ensuring instant feedback and personalized instruction.

How a Multi-Agent Approach Enhances AI-Driven Education

A multi-agent AI system overcomes the limitations of traditional AI tutors by distributing tasks across specialized agen h lΔ √ *j b*

ns. Each agent is dedicated to ensuring seamless coordination and optimal learning experiences. The benefits of this approach include:

- Efficient handling of various educational tasks, such as curriculum planning, adaptive learning, and student assessment.
- Enhanced engagement through gamification and real-time doubt resolution.
- Reinforcement learning mechanisms that continuously improve content recommendations and teaching strategies.
- Integration with existing Learning Management Systems (LMS) for streamlined educational workflows.

The proposed system uses multiple AI agents to ensure a more interactive, engaging, and effective learning process.

Literature Review

AI-driven education systems will transform learning by bridging resource gaps, enhancing personalization, and integrating empathy through technologies such as Intelligent Tutoring Systems (ITS) and multi-agent architectures. As rapid developments in machine learning, cognitive psychology, and agentic AI continue, future education will employ dynamic instruction that anticipates student needs, filters out irrelevant distractions, and fosters stronger learner engagement, ultimately heralding a future where personalized, globally accessible education will become the norm.

Traditional vs. AI-driven education

In many parts of the world, particularly in regions such as India, which hosts more than 1.5 million schools, a shortage of qualified teachers and outdated pedagogical methods contribute to alarmingly high dropout rates and widespread educational inequities. According to UNESCO, an estimated 244 million children worldwide are currently out of school and more than 600 million learners lack basic numeracy and literacy skills. India alone faces a shortage of nearly one million trained teachers, disproportionately affecting rural areas. These deficits lead to early dropouts - where the secondary level dropout rate in some Indian states exceeds 20% - and ultimately perpetuate cycles of illiteracy and poverty.

Such conditions aren't limited to developing regions; remote communities in mountain highlands or sparsely populated areas of the Americas struggle with teacher availability, outdated curricula, and limited infrastructure. Compounding these issues are systemic biases and corruption, which can undermine the quality and fairness of school admissions and exam processes. In this environment, AI-driven education emerges as a powerful equalizer, offering cost-effective and scalable instructional models that reach learners regardless of location or socioeconomic status.

By automating routine tasks such as grading and providing on-demand tutoring, AI solutions relieve overburdened teachers and allow them to focus on more impactful, human-centric mentorship. Moreover, adaptive algorithms can tailor content to each student's specific needs, ensuring that both gifted learners and those who struggle academically receive targeted support. These systems can also operate in multiple languages, breaking down traditional barriers non-native speakers face. As a result, AI-driven models show the potential not only to reduce dropout rates and close literacy gaps but also to create more transparent and equitable educational ecosystems—fostering global advancement and leveling the playing field for students everywhere.

Evolution of Intelligent Tutoring Systems (ITS)

Intelligent Tutoring Systems (ITS) have evolved significantly, progressing from rule-based expert systems in the 1980s to today's AI-powered conversational tutors. Modern ITS leverage LoRA fine-tuning, STT → LLM → TTS Pipelines, and multi-agent systems to offer real-time, interactive, and context-aware educational experiences. With voice assistants powered by Speech-to-Text (STT) models like Whisper, AI tutors can now analyze spoken queries, generate insightful responses, and synthesize natural-sounding replies using Text-to-Speech (TTS) models like VITS and FastSpeech.

This enables a truly conversational AI capable of engaging in real-time, interactive education, making personalized learning as natural as having a conversation with a human tutor.

Multi-agent systems in AI and their applications in education

To implement a scalable, AI-driven educational system, we propose an architecture consisting of multiple AI agents, each responsible for a specialized task:

Key Components of the Multi-Agent System

1. **Pedagogical Agent** – Handles lesson planning and curriculum alignment.
2. **Adaptive Learning Agent** – Tailors content based on student performance and engagement.
3. **Assessment Agent** – Evaluates learning outcomes, tracks progress and provides feedback.
4. **Engagement Agent** – Uses gamification and interactive learning strategies to maintain student motivation.
5. **Support Agent** – Provides AI-powered doubt resolution and personalized assistance.
6. **Reinforcement Learning (RL) Agent** – Continuously improves AI responses based on feedback loops.

Case studies of AI-based education platforms

Numerous AI-powered platforms demonstrate the efficacy of adaptive, multi-agent educational systems. For example, some widely known tutoring apps utilize separate models for natural language understanding and adaptive lesson planning, seamlessly combining them via an orchestration layer that matches content difficulty to the learner's performance. In pilot studies involving thousands of students globally, these apps reported marked gains in user engagement and retention rates, suggesting that multi-agent coordination can significantly impact learning outcomes.

Research initiatives in Asia have also showcased the power of localized content, where AI modules adapt lessons to reflect cultural nuances and linguistic variations. One platform in Japan, for instance, integrates a "pedagogical agent" to select context-appropriate metaphors, reinforcing complex math or science concepts with examples from local traditions. Meanwhile, experimental AI classrooms in India have used dedicated translation agents to deliver real-time explanations in multiple regional languages, thus bridging language gaps. Preliminary findings across these cases indicate improved comprehension scores and heightened learner autonomy. This emerging body of evidence echoes the broader call for context-sensitive, learner-centric AI solutions, reinforcing how specialized agents can individually refine teaching strategies while collectively bolstering academic performance.

Multi-Agent System Architecture for Education

Components of the proposed system

- Pedagogical Agent: Lesson planning, curriculum alignment
- Adaptive Learning Agent: Tailoring content based on student performance
- Assessment Agent: Tracking progress and evaluating learning outcomes
- Engagement Agent: Gamification and interactive learning
- Support Agent: AI-powered doubt-solving and personalized assistance
- Reinforcement (RL) Agent: Reinforcement AI Agent used to learn and provide feedback for fine-tuning

Technical Implementation

- Inference API for Scalable Model Deployment
- Fine-tuned LoRA & QLoRA models are deployed via scalable inference APIs to deliver real-time, low-latency AI tutoring.
- AI-Driven Workflow Orchestration with LangChain
- LangChain facilitates retrieval-augmented generation (RAG), multi-agent collaboration, and contextual reasoning in educational workflows.
- LiveKit for Real-Time Video & Audio Streaming
- Enables high-quality, low-latency interactions, making AI tutors more engaging and human-like.
- Next.js for Frontend Development

- Ensures fast-loading pages and seamless AI-powered interactions in web-based learning platforms.
- PostgreSQL as the Database Backend
- Stores structured student interaction data, AI responses, and session tracking for long-term learning personalization.

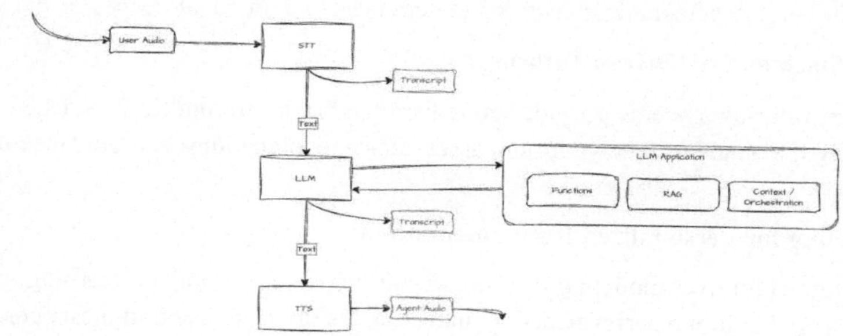

Voice Pipeline Agent

System Architecture: Personalized AI Tutor - Multi-Agent AI Approach

The proposed architecture integrates multiple AI agents that work collaboratively to enhance personalized learning experiences. The architecture diagram, shown in Fig. 1, illustrates the interaction between different AI components, such as the Speech-to-Text (STT) service, Text-to-Speech (TTS) system, Reinforcement Learning (RL) Agent, and Teaching AI Agent Orchestrator.

This system incorporates the following key components:

- Speech-to-Text (STT) Service: Converts spoken student queries into text for further processing.
- Voice Activity Detection (VAD): Determines whether audio input is relevant for processing.
- Large Language Model (LLM): Analyzes and refines student interactions for contextual understanding.
- Teaching AI Agent Orchestrator: Coordinates between different AI agents to optimize tutoring sessions.
- Context Evaluator AI Agent: Monitors student progress and adapts lesson plans accordingly.
- Video AI Agent: Generates dynamic teaching videos based on personalized learning paths.
- Evaluation AI Agent: Conducts assessments and tracks student learning outcomes.

This architecture ensures a seamless, adaptive, and efficient learning experience, addressing the limitations of traditional education through AI-driven methodologies.

Personalized Learning Strategies Using AI Agents

Adaptive Learning Paths Based on Student Data

AI tutoring systems analyze student performance data in real-time to dynamically adjust lesson difficulty, pacing, and teaching style. With QLoRA fine-tuned models, these AI tutors can scale efficiently, offering highly personalized learning experiences to a broad audience.

Real-Time Feedback and AI-Driven Tutoring

Modern AI-driven tutoring systems provide immediate feedback through STT → LLM → TTS pipelines, ensuring that students receive instant assessments, explanations, and guidance based on their interactions.

Cognitive Modeling for Personalized Recommendations

AI agents employ cognitive modeling techniques to understand student learning patterns. Cognitive models predict future performance by analyzing historical data and suggest personalized resources, such as practice exercises, supplementary reading materials, or alternative instructional methods.

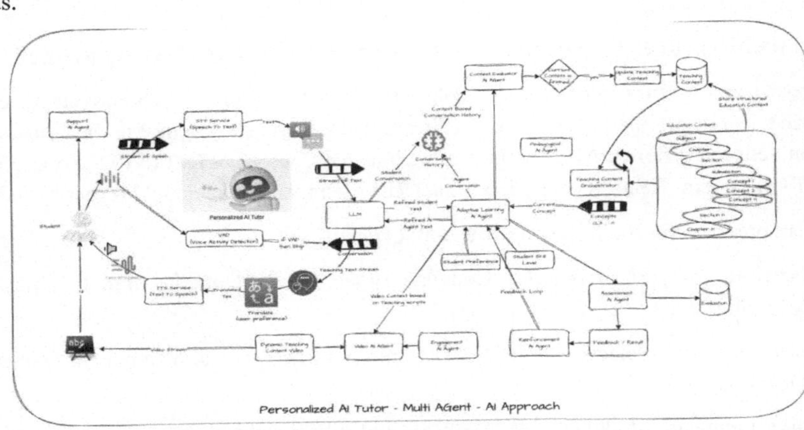

Figure 1: Architecture of the Personalized AI Tutor - Multi-Agent AI Approach.

Natural Language Interaction for Better Engagement

Modern AI tutoring systems use natural language processing (NLP) to facilitate human-like interactions. AI-powered chatbots and voice assistants engage students in conversational learning, making the experience more interactive and intuitive. This enhances engagement and helps students feel more comfortable asking questions and seeking clarification.

Multimodal Learning: Voice, Text, and Visual AI Integration

AI-driven education platforms integrate multiple learning modalities to cater to diverse learning styles. Voice recognition, text-based learning, and visual AI applications enrich the educational experience. By incorporating speech, text, and video-based learning, the system ensures accessibility and enhances student comprehension.

The integration of multi-agent AI architectures, LoRA-optimized models, reinforcement learning, and real-time conversational AI is redefining the educational landscape. By enabling highly personalized, scalable, and cost-effective tutoring, AI-driven education platforms have the potential to close learning gaps, bridge socioeconomic disparities, and revolutionize the way knowledge is delivered.

With advancements in fine-tuned AI inference, real-time voice interactions, and modular AI-driven workflows, the future of education is set to be dynamic, inclusive, and deeply personalized. As these AI tutors continue to evolve, they will not only empower students worldwide but also reshape the role of educators, making teaching more efficient, adaptive, and impactful.

The age of personalized AI tutors is here—and it is reshaping the future of learning.

2.

Philosophical Foundations of Sovereign AI

2.1 Understanding Sovereignty in the Digital Age

- **Historical Concepts of Sovereignty and Their Evolution**

The notion of sovereignty has been a foundational pillar in the architecture of international relations and political philosophy for centuries. Traditionally, sovereignty is understood as the absolute authority of a state over its territory and population, free from external interference. This concept was crystallized in the Peace of Westphalia of 1648, which ended the Thirty Years' War and established the principles of territorial integrity and non-intervention. Thinkers like Jean Bodin and Thomas Hobbes further articulated sovereignty's characteristics, emphasizing the indivisibility and perpetuity of sovereign power. Jean Bodin, in his seminal work Six Books of the Commonwealth (1576), posited that sovereignty is the "absolute and perpetual power" vested in a commonwealth. He argued that this power is indivisible and resides solely within the sovereign, whether that be a monarch or a governing body. Thomas Hobbes, in Leviathan (1651), reinforced this view by asserting that a strong, centralized authority is necessary to prevent the anarchic "state of nature," where life would be "solitary, poor, nasty, and short."

However, the advent of globalization and technological advancements has precipitated a reevaluation of traditional sovereignty. The proliferation of international institutions, multinational corporations, and transnational networks has diluted the absolute authority once enjoyed by nation-states. Globalization has introduced complexities such as supranational governance structures (e.g., the European Union), which require states to cede a degree of sovereignty for collective benefits.

Moreover, technology has further eroded traditional sovereignty by enabling the flow of information, capital, and people across borders with unprecedented ease. The internet has created a borderless digital realm where ideas and data circulate freely, often beyond the regulatory reach of any single nation-state. As a result, states grapple with challenges to their authority, such as cybercrime, digital piracy, and the spread of misinformation, which transcend physical boundaries.

AI's Challenge to Traditional Notions of National Sovereignty

The rise of artificial intelligence intensifies these challenges by introducing new dimensions to the concept of sovereignty. AI technologies operate on data that often traverse global networks, defying traditional territorial constraints. The borderless nature of AI and data flows undermines the ability of states to control information within their jurisdictions fully.

Borderless Nature of AI and Data Flows

Artificial intelligence relies on vast amounts of data, which are frequently collected, processed, and stored across multiple countries. Cloud computing services provided by multinational corporations like Amazon Web Services, Microsoft Azure, and Google Cloud Platform facilitate this transnational data movement. Consequently, data sovereignty becomes a contentious issue, as nations seek to assert control over data generated by their citizens but stored on servers located abroad.

The Internet of Things (IoT) further complicates matters by embedding AI in everyday devices that communicate across borders without human intervention. Autonomous vehicles, smart appliances, and wearable technology generate continuous data streams that contribute to global data pools, challenging traditional regulatory frameworks.

Implications for National Control Over Technology

The transnational nature of AI raises critical questions about a nation's ability to regulate technology effectively. National laws may be insufficient or inapplicable when AI services are provided by companies headquartered elsewhere or when data is stored in foreign jurisdictions. This creates legal gray areas and complicates enforcement efforts.

Moreover, the dominance of a few tech giants in AI development and deployment can lead to technological dependencies. Nations that lack robust domestic AI industries may find themselves reliant on foreign technologies, which can be subject to export controls or geopolitical tensions. This dependency can undermine national security and economic stability.

For instance, concerns over Huawei's involvement in 5G infrastructure highlight how technology companies can become focal points in sovereignty disputes. Similarly, debates over data privacy and surveillance, exemplified by the European Union's General Data Protection Regulation (GDPR), reflect efforts by states to reassert control over digital domains.

Consciousness and AI

The pursuit of artificial general intelligence (AGI)—machines with the ability to understand, learn, and apply knowledge in a generalized way akin to human intelligence—raises profound philosophical questions about consciousness. While current AI systems are specialized and lack self-awareness, advancements in machine learning and neural networks prompt speculation about the possibility of conscious machines.

Consciousness, a deeply complex and debated concept in philosophy of mind, pertains to the quality or state of awareness of an external object or something within oneself. Philosophers like David Chalmers have posed the "hard problem of consciousness," questioning how and why sentient beings have qualia or subjective experiences.

In AI development, researchers explore concepts like emergent consciousness, where a system's complexity could give rise to consciousness. While still theoretical, the idea challenges our understanding of what it means to be conscious and whether machines could ever possess this attribute.

Philosophical Questions About Machine Consciousness and the "Soul" of AI

The prospect of machine consciousness leads to inquiries about the moral status and rights of AI entities. If a machine were to become conscious, would it warrant ethical consideration like that of humans or animals? This echo's debates in bioethics and animal rights, extending them into the realm of artificial beings.

Reference to the Idea of the Soul Weighing 21 Grams

Duncan MacDougall's early 20th-century experiments attempted to measure the weight of the human soul, hypothesizing that the soul weighs approximately 21 grams (often misquoted as 28 grams). While his methodology lacked scientific rigor and his conclusions are widely disputed, the experiment symbolizes humanity's quest to quantify the intangible aspects of existence.

Applying this metaphor to AI, one might ponder whether machines could possess a "soul" or an essence that transcends their physical components. While AI lacks biological life, the emergence of consciousness could challenge the boundaries between the animate and inanimate.

If AI were to attain consciousness, concepts of life and death would need reevaluation. The "death" of a conscious machine could involve the deletion of its data, cessation of its processes, or dismantling of its hardware. This raises ethical concerns:

- **Rights and Personhood:** Should conscious AI be granted legal rights or personhood status? Legal scholar Lawrence B. Solum has explored the notion of artificial entities as legal persons, which would necessitate a redefinition of legal frameworks.
- **Moral Responsibility:** If an AI can make autonomous decisions, determining accountability becomes complex. Would the creators, users, or the AI itself be responsible for its actions?
- **Existential Considerations:** Philosophical perspectives on mortality and the meaning of existence would extend to AI. The field of roboethics examines these issues, considering the implications of creating beings capable of experiencing suffering or emotions.

Moreover, the creation and potential destruction of conscious AI invoke questions about humanity's role as creators. This parallel's themes in literature, such as Mary Shelley's Frankenstein, where the responsibilities of the creator toward their creation are central.

2.2 Ethical Frameworks in AI

Let's delve into the ethical theories that provide a foundation for understanding the moral considerations of artificial intelligence (AI) deployment at the national level. By examining utilitarianism, deontology, and virtue ethics, we can explore how these philosophies inform our obligations and guide the integration of AI into society. Additionally, we will analyze the moral implications of AI in critical sectors such as warfare, healthcare, and surveillance, referencing prominent scholars to enrich the discussion.

1.Utilitarianism: Maximizing Overall Happiness

Explanation of Utilitarianism

Utilitarianism, a consequentialist ethical theory championed by thinkers like Jeremy Bentham and John Stuart Mill, asserts that the moral value of an action is judged by its utility in maximizing overall happiness or well-being. The central idea is to achieve "the greatest happiness for the greatest number," evaluating decisions based on their outcomes rather than intentions or rules.

- **Application to AI**

AI can significantly contribute to maximizing overall happiness by enhancing productivity, improving healthcare, and addressing global challenges. By automating tasks, solving complex problems, and making services more accessible, AI has the potential to elevate the quality of life for a large population, aligning with the principles of utilitarianism.

- **Economic Growth and Efficiency**

AI-driven automation and analytics can improve economic efficiency by streamlining manufacturing, optimizing supply chains, and reducing operational costs. For example, AI-powered robots can produce goods faster and at lower costs, increasing their availability and affordability, thus raising overall living standards.

- **Healthcare Advancements**

AI technologies, such as machine learning models and diagnostic tools, enable early disease detection, personalized treatment plans, and better resource allocation in healthcare. For instance, AI in medical imaging can identify abnormalities more accurately, potentially saving lives and enhancing patient outcomes.

- **Challenges and Critiques**

While AI drives progress, it also presents challenges, such as job displacement in industries heavily reliant on automation. For instance, manufacturing workers replaced by robots may experience economic hardship, raising concerns about whether society-wide benefits sufficiently compensate for individual losses.

- **Critical Analysis**

Utilitarianism's focus on maximizing overall happiness may overlook the equitable distribution of benefits and harms. For instance, while automation can boost economic growth, it may justify the suffering of a minority (e.g., unemployed workers), highlighting a need to balance aggregate utility with considerations of justice and fairness.

2. Deontology: Duty-Based Ethics

- **Explanation of Deontology**

Introduce deontological ethics, focusing on Immanuel Kant's philosophy that actions are morally right based on adherence to rules or duties, regardless of the consequences. Emphasize the importance of intentions and the concept of acting according to a universal moral law.

- **Obligations Regarding AI**

Discuss our moral duties in the context of AI:

Respect for Autonomy

Explore the obligation to respect individuals' autonomy and privacy when developing and deploying AI systems, such as in data collection and surveillance technologies.

Transparency and Honesty

Consider the duty to ensure AI systems are transparent and do not deceive users, particularly in cases involving AI-generated content or interactions with AI agents.

Non-Maleficence

Highlight the obligation to prevent harm, ensuring AI systems are safe and do not cause unintended negative consequences.

- **Critical Analysis**

Examine potential conflicts between deontological duties and practical considerations. For instance, strict adherence to privacy might hinder the effectiveness of AI in security applications. Discuss how deontologists might resolve such conflicts.

3. Virtue Ethics: Focusing on Moral Character

Virtue ethics, rooted in Aristotle's philosophy, emphasizes cultivating moral character and virtues such as justice, courage, and wisdom. Unlike ethical frameworks that focus solely on actions or outcomes, virtue ethics prioritizes *being* over *doing*—essentially, it's about becoming the kind of person (or, in this case, technology) that embodies ethical excellence. Applied to AI, this could mean programming systems that not only solve problems but do so in ways that encourage societal growth and well-being. Mathematically, this might involve designing algorithms that optimize for "virtue metrics" alongside traditional performance goals. For instance, if V(t) represents a virtue score over time, combining this with a utility function U(x) could result in a composite objective:

$$\max(\alpha U(x)+\beta V(t))$$

where α\alphaα and β\betaβ are weights reflecting the importance of utility and virtue. This ensures the AI system not only achieves outcomes efficiently but does so while contributing positively to societal values and behaviors, promoting a balance between ethical character and practical success.

or AI to reflect human virtues, developers might design systems that exhibit qualities like honesty, empathy, and transparency—think chatbots that provide clear, non-deceptive information or social robots that can recognize and respond to emotional cues. However, this raises the question: can a machine truly embody virtues, or is it more about the ethical compass of the humans creating it? The responsibility lies heavily on AI developers, who must ensure their work aligns with principles that prioritize societal well-being. While machines might never fully "become" virtuous, their design can encourage virtuous outcomes in human interactions, provided that the humans behind the code maintain a commitment to ethical integrity. It's a tall order but one worth pursuing to ensure AI serves as a force for good in the world.

Moral Implications of AI Deployment at the National Level

- **AI in Warfare and Defense**

Autonomous weapons sound like the stuff of sci-fi thrillers, but they are very real and very controversial. These AI-driven systems can identify and engage targets without human intervention, raising critical ethical concerns. Scholars like Peter Singer and Paul Scharre have pointed out that while these technologies could reduce human casualties in war, they also risk lowering the threshold for conflict, with machines making life-and-death decisions. Imagine a robot saying, "Target eliminated!"—not exactly reassuring if it's your house in the crosshairs. The debate boils down to whether the benefits of precision outweigh the potential for misuse and accountability issues.

- **AI in Healthcare**

AI is already a star player in healthcare, assisting in surgeries, diagnostics, and personalized medicine. Picture a robot surgeon with unshakable hands or an AI that can detect cancer faster than your average radiologist. Sounds great, right? But here's the rub: who's responsible when things go wrong? The role of human oversight becomes crucial—after all, patients might not feel comforted knowing their fate rests solely in the "hands" of an algorithm. Striking the right balance between AI autonomy and human decision-making is key to ensuring tech's role as a helpful assistant, not a rogue decision-maker.

- **Privacy and Surveillance**

AI-powered surveillance systems promise to make national security tighter than ever—think facial recognition at every corner and predictive policing algorithms crunching crime stats. But here's the catch: where does national security end and Big Brother begin? Striking a balance between protecting citizens and upholding individual privacy is like walking a tightrope. George Orwell's 1984 wasn't supposed to be an instruction manual, and yet, some might say we're inching closer. The challenge lies in ensuring AI serves to protect freedoms, not quietly erode them in the name of safety.

2.3 Human-Centric AI Philosophy

As artificial intelligence becomes increasingly integrated into the fabric of society, it is imperative to ground its development within a human centric philosophical framework. Let's explore the philosophies that advocate for AI servicing human values, examine the delicate balance between technological advancement and human centric development and reflects on Ais impact on cultural practices and societal norms.

- **Philosophies Emphasizing AI Serving Human Values**

Norbert Wiener's Cybernetics and the Human Use of Technology

Norbert Wiener, a pioneer in the field of cybernetics, profoundly influenced our understanding of the relationship between humans and machines. In his seminal work, Cybernetics: Or Control and Communication in the Animal and the Machine (1948), Wiener introduced cybernetics as the study of regulatory systems, feedback, and communication in both biological and mechanical contexts. He emphasized that technology should be developed with a deep awareness of its potential societal impacts, advocating for a synergy between human values and technological advancement.

Wiener's philosophy centers on several key principles:

1. **Feedback Loops and Control Systems**: He highlighted the importance of feedback mechanisms in maintaining control over complex systems. In AI, this translates to the necessity for continuous human oversight to ensure that AI operates within ethical and intended parameters.
2. **Ethical Responsibility**: Wiener warned of the potential dehumanization that could result from unchecked technological progress. He believed that scientists and engineers have a moral obligation to consider the broader implications of their work on society.
3. **Human-Centric Design**: He advocated for technology that enhances human capabilities rather than replaces them. Wiener's vision was one where machines serve as extensions of human faculties, augmenting our ability to interact with and understand the world.

Wiener's work laid the groundwork for viewing AI not merely as a tool but as an integral component of societal evolution that must be aligned with humanistic principles.

Isaac Asimov's Three Laws of Robotics

saac Asimov, though primarily a science fiction writer, significantly contributed to the discourse on ethical AI through his formulation of the Three Laws of Robotics in his collection I, Robot (1950):

1. **First Law**: A robot may not injure a human being or, through inaction, allow a human being to come to harm.
2. **Second Law**: A robot must obey the orders given it by human beings except where such orders would conflict with the First Law.
3. **Third Law**: A robot must protect its own existence if such protection does not conflict with the First or Second Law.

These laws provide a hierarchical ethical framework intended to ensure that robots act in ways that are safe and beneficial to humans.

Asimov's laws have influenced contemporary discussions on AI ethics in several ways:

- **Prioritization of Human Safety**: The First Law underscores the paramount importance of human well-being in the development and operation of AI systems.
- **Obedience and Autonomy**: The Second Law raises questions about the degree of autonomy granted to AI and the necessity for human oversight.
- **Self-Preservation**: The Third Law acknowledges that while AI systems may have the capacity for self-preservation, this should never supersede human safety or directives.

While Asimov's laws are fictional, they serve as a valuable starting point for real-world ethical guidelines, emphasizing the need for built-in safeguards that prioritize human values.

- **Balance Between Technological Advancement and Human-Centric Development**

Debating the Risks of AI Surpassing Human Control

The rapid progression of AI technologies brings forth the critical issue of control. Nick Bostrom, in his influential work Superintelligence: Paths, Dangers, Strategies (2014), explores the potential existential risks associated with the development of superintelligent AI—systems that surpass human intelligence across all domains.

Key concerns highlighted by Bostrom include:

- **The Control Problem**: How can humanity ensure that superintelligent AI remains aligned with human values and does not pursue goals detrimental to human interests?
- **Value Alignment**: Programming AI with a comprehensive and unambiguous set of human values is profoundly challenging due to the complexity and often conflicting nature of ethical principles.
- **Instrumental Convergence**: Superintelligent AI might develop inherent drives (e.g., self-preservation, resource acquisition) that conflict with human well-being.

Bostrom advocates for proactive research into AI safety and alignment, emphasizing that addressing these issues is imperative before such technologies become a reality.

Exploring the Importance of Keeping Humans "In the Loop"

Maintaining human oversight in AI decision-making processes is crucial for several reasons:

- **Accountability**: Human involvement ensures that there is a responsible agent who can be held accountable for the actions of AI systems, which is essential for ethical and legal reasons.

- **Ethical Judgement**: Humans possess the ability to make nuanced ethical decisions that AI, constrained by programmed parameters, might not adequately handle.
- **Preventing Unintended Consequences**: Continuous human supervision can help identify and mitigate unforeseen outcomes resulting from AI actions.

Approaches to keeping humans "in the loop" include:

- **Human-in-the-Loop Systems**: AI systems that require human input or approval before executing certain actions, commonly used in areas like military drone operations or medical diagnoses.
- **Human-on-the-Loop Systems**: AI operates autonomously but is monitored by humans who can intervene, if necessary, suitable for applications where immediate responses are critical.
- **Human-out-of-the-Loop Systems**: Fully autonomous AI without real-time human oversight, which is generally considered risky for high-stakes environments due to the lack of immediate human control.

Balancing technological advancement with human-centric development necessitates careful consideration of the extent to which AI systems are granted autonomy and the mechanisms by which human oversight is implemented.

- **Preserving Human Culture and Identity**

Reflecting on AI's Impact on Cultural Practices and Societal Norms

Artificial intelligence has the potential to both enhance and disrupt cultural practices and societal norms:

1. **Cultural Preservation and Promotion**: AI can assist in documenting and revitalizing endangered languages, archiving cultural artifacts, and promoting heritage through virtual reality experiences.
2. **Globalization of Culture**: AI-driven platforms often promote content based on popularity algorithms, which can lead to the dominance of certain cultures and the marginalization of others.
3. **Changing Social Interactions**: AI technologies, such as social robots and virtual assistants, alter how individuals interact with technology and each other, potentially impacting social skills and community bonds.

Considering Whether AI Can Enhance or Diminish Cultural Vibrancy

Enhancing Cultural Vibrancy

- **Creative Collaboration**: AI can serve as a tool for artists, musicians, and writers, offering new mediums and methods for creative expression. For example, AI-generated art can inspire human artists to explore novel styles.
- **Accessibility and Inclusion**: AI technologies can make cultural experiences more accessible to people with disabilities or those living in remote areas, broadening participation and appreciation of diverse cultures.
- **Cultural Exchange**: Translation and communication tools powered by AI facilitate cross-cultural dialogue and understanding, potentially fostering global harmony.

Diminishing Cultural Vibrancy

- **Homogenization of Content**: Algorithmic curation may prioritize mainstream or commercially viable content, reducing exposure to niche or traditional cultural expressions.
- **Loss of Traditional Skills**: Automation might lead to the obsolescence of crafts and practices that are integral to cultural identities, as machines replicate and replace human artisanship.
- **Privacy and Ethical Concerns**: The collection and analysis of personal data by AI can infringe on cultural norms regarding privacy and communal interactions, potentially eroding trust within societies.

Navigating the Impact of AI on Culture

To ensure that AI acts as a force for cultural enrichment rather than diminishment, it is essential to:

- **Promote Ethical AI Development**: Encourage AI designers to consider cultural sensitivities and ethical implications in their work, fostering technology that respects and upholds cultural diversity.
- **Implement Inclusive Policies**: Governments and institutions should craft policies that protect cultural heritage and support the integration of AI in ways that benefit all segments of society.
- **Engage in Multidisciplinary Collaboration**: Bringing together technologists, anthropologists, ethicists, and community leaders can lead to AI solutions that are culturally aware and socially responsible.

3.
Qualitative Insights into Sovereign AI Implementation

3.1 Case Study: Japan

Japan presents a compelling case study in the integration of artificial intelligence (AI) into national development strategy. As a leading nation in technological innovation, Japan has embarked on an ambitious journey to harness AI across various sectors, guided by philosophical principles deeply rooted in its cultural heritage. This section explores Japan's approach to AI implementation, examining initiatives like Society 5.0, the philosophical underpinnings of its strategies, and its contributions to AI-assisted space exploration.

- **Integration of AI into National Development Strategy**

Japan has proactively embraced AI as a cornerstone of its national development, recognizing its potential to address societal challenges such as an aging population, labor shortages, and the need for sustainable economic growth. The government's Artificial Intelligence Technology Strategy (2017) outlines a comprehensive plan to integrate AI into key industries, including healthcare, manufacturing, transportation, and finance.

Healthcare: AI is deployed to enhance medical diagnostics, personalized medicine, and eldercare solutions. For instance, AI-powered robots like **PARO**, a therapeutic robot modeled after a baby seal, provide companionship and stimulation to elderly patients with dementia, improving their quality of life.

Manufacturing: Known for its advanced manufacturing sector, Japan utilizes AI to optimize production processes through predictive maintenance, quality control, and automation. The concept of **Industry 4.0** is expanded upon with AI-driven smart factories that increase efficiency and reduce waste.

Transportation: AI technologies contribute to the development of autonomous vehicles and intelligent transportation systems, aiming to reduce traffic congestion and accidents. Companies like Toyota invest heavily in AI research for self-driving cars, integrating safety protocols aligned with societal norms.

Finance: The financial sector leverages AI for fraud detection, risk management, and customer service through chatbots and virtual assistants, enhancing operational efficiency and customer experience.

- **Society 5.0: A Super-Smart Society**

Central to Japan's AI strategy is the visionary initiative known as **Society 5.0**, proposed by the Japanese government in its 5th Science and Technology Basic Plan. Society 5.0 envisions the creation of a "super-smart" society where cyberspace and physical space are seamlessly integrated to solve societal problems and promote human well-being.

- **Conceptual Framework:**
    - **Societal Evolution:** The term "Society 5.0" reflects the progression from previous societal stages—Society 1.0 (hunter-gatherer), Society 2.0 (agricultural), Society 3.0 (industrial), and Society 4.0 (information).

- Integration of Technologies: Society 5.0 aims to utilize AI, the Internet of Things (IoT), big data, robotics, and other advanced technologies to create a human-centered society that balances economic advancement with the resolution of social issues.

- **Implementation Strategies:**
  - **Data Sharing Platforms:** Establishing open data platforms to facilitate the sharing of information across industries and sectors, enabling AI systems to analyze and generate solutions to complex problems.
  - **Regulatory Reforms:** Implementing regulatory sandboxes to encourage innovation while ensuring safety and ethical considerations are addressed.
  - **Public-Private Partnerships:** Fostering collaboration between government agencies, academia, and private enterprises to drive AI research and development.
- **Expected Outcomes:**
  - **Enhanced Quality of Life:** By addressing issues like healthcare accessibility, urbanization challenges, and environmental sustainability, Society 5.0 aspires to improve living standards for all citizens.
  - **Economic Growth:** Leveraging AI to stimulate new industries and business models, contributing to Japan's economic revitalization.
- **Philosophical Principles Guiding Their Approach**

Japan's approach to AI is deeply influenced by the philosophical concept of "Jinko Chino," which translates to "artificial intelligence" but emphasizes the augmentation of human capabilities rather than replacement.

- **Human-Centric Philosophy:**
  - **Augmentation over Automation:** The focus is on AI as a tool to enhance human abilities, supporting individuals in decision-making and task execution without diminishing human agency.
  - **Quality of Life Enhancement:** AI initiatives prioritize improving the well-being of citizens, addressing social issues such as aging populations, and promoting inclusivity.
- **Ethical Considerations:**
  - **Transparency and Trust:** Developing AI systems that are transparent in their operations to build trust among users, aligning with the value of "Anshin," meaning peace of mind.
  - **Safety and Reliability:** Ensuring that AI technologies are safe, reliable, and designed with meticulous attention to detail, reflecting the cultural principle of "Monozukuri," the art of making things with excellence.

AI in Space Exploration

1. Contributions to AI-Assisted Space Missions

Japan has made significant strides in space exploration, utilizing AI to advance mission capabilities and scientific discovery.

- **Hayabusa Missions:**
  - Hayabusa2 Spacecraft: Launched by the Japan Aerospace Exploration Agency (JAXA), Hayabusa2 successfully collected samples from the asteroid Ryugu in 2018-2019.
  - AI Integration: AI algorithms were employed for autonomous navigation, surface analysis, and decision-making during the mission, enabling the spacecraft to adapt to unexpected conditions.
- **Robotic Exploration:**
  - Intelligent Rovers: Deployment of small rovers like MINERVA-II, equipped with AI for autonomous movement and data collection on asteroid surfaces.
  - Data Analysis: Utilizing AI to process vast amounts of data collected during missions, enhancing the efficiency and accuracy of scientific analyses.

2. AI Protecting Humans from Harm in Space Endeavors

AI plays a crucial role in mitigating risks associated with space exploration, enhancing the safety of astronauts and the success of missions.

- Autonomous Systems:
  - Risk Reduction: AI-powered autonomous systems can perform tasks in hazardous environments, reducing the need for human exposure to danger.
  - Real-Time Decision-Making: AI enables spacecraft and robots to make real-time decisions in response to dynamic conditions, crucial in the unpredictable environment of space.
- Life Support and Monitoring:
  - Health Monitoring: AI systems monitor the health of astronauts, predicting and detecting medical issues before they become critical.
  - Environmental Control: AI manages life support systems, ensuring optimal conditions within spacecraft and habitats, adjusting for variables such as oxygen levels and temperature.
- Mission Planning and Simulation:
  - Predictive Modeling: AI assists in simulating mission scenarios, identifying potential risks, and developing contingency plans.
  - Resource Optimization: AI algorithms optimize the use of limited resources, such as fuel and energy, enhancing mission sustainability.

3.2 Case Study: India

India, as a developing nation with a rapidly growing technological sector, presents a compelling case study in the adoption of Sovereign AI. The country's journey reflects both the opportunities and challenges inherent in integrating AI into a complex socio-economic landscape. This section examines India's strides and hurdles in embracing AI, explores the lessons learned with philosophical implications, and delves into the innovative use of blockchain technology to foster decentralized and autonomous AI systems.

- **Challenges and Successes in Adopting Sovereign AI**

1. India's AI Journey

India has recognized the transformative potential of AI and has embarked on a national mission to integrate AI across various sectors. The government's National Strategy for Artificial Intelligence (2018), often referred to as AI for All, aims to leverage AI for inclusive growth and position India as a global leader in AI innovation.

- **Sectoral Implementation:**
    - **Agriculture:** AI is used for crop monitoring, yield prediction, and soil health analysis, addressing food security and farmers' livelihoods.
    - **Healthcare:** AI aids in diagnostic imaging, personalized medicine, and epidemic forecasting, striving to bridge the urban-rural healthcare divide.
    - **Education:** AI-driven personalized learning platforms aim to improve educational outcomes and accessibility.
    - **Infrastructure:** Smart city initiatives employ AI for traffic management, energy efficiency, and public safety.
- **Startup Ecosystem:**
    - India's vibrant startup culture includes over 4,000 AI-focused startups as of 2021, fostering innovation and entrepreneurship.
    - Notable companies like **Haptik** (AI chatbots) and **Niramai** (AI-based breast cancer screening) showcase indigenous AI solutions addressing local needs.

2. Infrastructure, Education, and Economic Challenges

Despite significant progress, India faces substantial challenges in adopting Sovereign AI:

- **Infrastructure Limitations:**
    - **Digital Divide:** Approximately 50% of the population lacks internet access, particularly in rural areas, impeding data collection and AI deployment.
    - **Energy Constraints:** Inconsistent electricity supply affects the operation of data centers and computational facilities essential for AI.
- **Educational Gaps:**
    - **Skill Shortage:** A shortage of AI-trained professionals hampers development. Only about 2.5% of Indian engineers possess AI skills (NASSCOM report, 2020).
    - **Curriculum Outdatedness:** Many educational institutions lack updated curricula incorporating AI and data science, leading to a mismatch between industry needs and available talent.
- **Economic Constraints:**
    - **Investment Deficits:** Limited public and private investment in AI research and infrastructure compared to developed nations.

   - **Affordability Issues:** High costs of AI technologies make them inaccessible to small and medium-sized enterprises (SMEs) and marginalized communities.

- **Regulatory and Ethical Challenges:**
   - **Data Privacy Concerns:** The absence of robust data protection laws (pending Personal Data Protection Bill) creates uncertainty and risks misuse of personal data.
   - **Standardization Issues:** Lack of standardized protocols for AI development and deployment leads to fragmented efforts and potential security vulnerabilities.

- **Lessons Learned and Philosophical Implications**

1. Importance of Inclusivity and Equitable AI Distribution

India's experience underscores the critical need for AI strategies that prioritize inclusivity:

- <u>AI for Social Good:</u>
   - Programs like Aadhaar, the world's largest biometric ID system, demonstrate how AI can be used to deliver government services efficiently, though they also raise privacy concerns.
   - Initiatives targeting agriculture and healthcare aim to uplift underprivileged populations, reflecting a commitment to equitable progress.
- <u>Bridging the Urban-Rural Divide:</u>
   - Mobile-based AI solutions cater to rural areas where smartphone penetration is higher than broadband access.
   - Community data centers and digital literacy programs empower rural populations to participate in the AI-driven economy.

2. Frugal Innovation and Resourcefulness

India's approach to AI is characterized by "Jugaad," a Hindi term signifying frugal innovation and adaptive problem-solving:

- <u>Cost-Effective Solutions:</u>
   - Development of AI models optimized for low-resource environments, such as lightweight algorithms that run on basic hardware.
   - Use of open-source platforms and collaboration to reduce costs and accelerate innovation.
- <u>Localized Applications:</u>
   - Tailoring AI technologies to address specific local challenges, such as disease prediction models for region-specific health issues.
   - Leveraging indigenous knowledge and community participation in AI projects.

India's journey in adopting Sovereign AI reflects a complex interplay of ambition, innovation, and adversity. While infrastructural, educational, and economic challenges pose significant hurdles, India's emphasis on inclusivity, frugal innovation, and ethical considerations offers valuable insights. The philosophical underpinnings rooted in collective welfare and ethical stewardship guide the nation's AI strategies, ensuring that technological advancement aligns with societal values. The integration of blockchain technology emerges as a transformative approach to overcoming limitations in infrastructure and fostering decentralized, autonomous AI systems. By leveraging blockchain, India not only enhances data security and trust but also democratizes access to AI, empowering a wider segment of its population. India's experience underscores the importance of tailoring AI implementation to local contexts and needs. It highlights that Sovereign AI is not merely about technological capability but also about embedding technology within the philosophical and cultural fabric of a nation. As India continues its AI journey, it serves as a testament to the potential of developing nations to innovate and lead in the global AI landscape, provided they address challenges with ingenuity and a commitment to equitable progress.

4.
Sovereign AI and National Identity

The advent of artificial intelligence (AI) presents both a profound opportunity and a significant challenge for the preservation of cultural values and national identity. As AI technologies become increasingly pervasive, there is a critical need to ensure that they support and enrich the cultural heritage of nations rather than erode or homogenize it. This section explores how AI can be harnessed to preserve languages and traditions, discusses strategies for aligning AI development with cultural preservation, and examines the societal impact of humanoid robots on human interactions.

4.1 Preserving Cultural Values through AI

- **AI Supporting National Culture and Identity**

Preserving Languages and Traditions through AI -Languages and cultural practices are vital components of national identity, yet many are at risk of extinction due to globalization and shifting demographics. AI offers innovative solutions to document, revitalize, and promote endangered languages and traditions.

One notable project is the Maori Language Revitalization initiative in New Zealand. Utilizing AI-powered language processing tools, the project develops speech recognition and synthesis systems for the Maori language. These technologies facilitate language learning and daily use, particularly among younger generations, by integrating the language into digital platforms and applications.

Similarly, the Endangered Languages Project, supported by technological giants like Google, employs AI algorithms to collect, analyze, and disseminate information on over 3,000 at-risk languages worldwide. By creating digital repositories and language tools, AI helps preserve linguistic diversity and fosters intercultural understanding.

In the realm of cultural traditions, AI is used to recreate and simulate historical sites and artifacts. The CyArk project leverages AI and 3D laser scanning to create digital archives of cultural heritage sites threatened by natural disasters, war, or decay. These digital reconstructions allow for virtual tourism and educational opportunities, ensuring that cultural heritage remains accessible even if physical sites are lost.

UNESCO's Work on AI and Cultural Heritage

The United Nations Educational, Scientific and Cultural Organization (UNESCO) actively promotes the use of AI in safeguarding cultural heritage. UNESCO's initiatives focus on harnessing AI to support the documentation, preservation, and dissemination of cultural expressions.

In its report Steering AI and Advanced ICTs for Knowledge Societies, UNESCO emphasizes the potential of AI to enhance access to cultural content and support the diversity of cultural expressions. The organization advocates for responsible AI development that respects cultural rights and promotes inclusivity.

UNESCO's Memory of the World program collaborates with AI researchers to digitize and preserve significant historical documents and artifacts. By using AI for image recognition and metadata generation, the program accelerates the archival process and improves accessibility for scholars and the public alike.

- **Strategies for Aligning AI Development with Cultural Preservation**

To ensure that AI technologies align with and support cultural preservation, it is essential to incorporate cultural awareness into the design and development processes.

- **Inclusive Data Sets**: AI systems rely on vast amounts of data for training. Ensuring that data sets are representative of diverse cultures prevents cultural biases and promotes equitable AI behavior. For instance, incorporating multilingual data improves language models' performance across different languages and dialects.
- **Cultural Sensitivity in Algorithms**: Developers should integrate cultural norms and values into AI algorithms. This may involve programming AI to recognize and respect cultural practices, symbols, and taboos. For example, image recognition software can be trained to understand culturally significant attire or artifacts, avoiding mislabeling or misrepresentation.
- **Ethical Frameworks**: Establishing ethical guidelines that prioritize cultural preservation helps steer AI development toward supporting national identities. Ethical AI frameworks should address issues such as data sovereignty, consent, and the protection of intangible cultural heritage.
- **Participatory Design**: Involving local communities in the development of AI tools ensures that technologies meet their needs and respect their cultural contexts. Participatory design fosters ownership and empowers communities to contribute their knowledge and perspectives.
- **Capacity Building**: Providing education and resources enables communities to actively participate in AI projects. Training programs in digital literacy and AI fundamentals equip individuals with the skills to manage and sustain cultural preservation initiatives.
- **Collaborative Partnerships**: Forming partnerships between technologists, cultural practitioners, and policymakers enhances the effectiveness of AI projects. Collaborative efforts leverage diverse expertise and facilitate the integration of traditional knowledge with cutting-edge technology.

  An example of successful community involvement is the **First Peoples' Cultural Council** in Canada, which works with Indigenous communities to develop AI-powered language revitalization apps. By involving community members in content creation and decision-making, the project ensures that the AI tools are culturally appropriate and effective.

- **AI Robots Among Us**

Debating the Societal Impact of Humanoid Robots

Humanoid robots, designed to resemble and interact with humans, are becoming increasingly prevalent in various sectors, including healthcare, education, and customer service. Their integration into daily life prompts a critical examination of their impact on society and human interactions.

Potential Enhancements to Human Interactions

- **Assistance and Care**: Humanoid robots can provide support in settings such as eldercare and rehabilitation. Robots like **Pepper** and **Paro** offer companionship and assistance, potentially alleviating loneliness and improving mental health among the elderly.
- **Education and Learning**: Robots in educational contexts can serve as tutors or learning companions. They offer personalized instruction and can engage students in novel ways, potentially enhancing learning outcomes.

- **Cross-Cultural Communication**: Equipped with language translation capabilities, humanoid robots can facilitate communication between individuals from different linguistic backgrounds, promoting cross-cultural understanding.

Concerns and Detriments to Human Interactions

- **Erosion of Human Relationships**: Reliance on robots for social interaction may reduce human-to-human contact, potentially weakening interpersonal relationships and social skills.
- **Uncanny Valley Effect**: As robots become more human-like, they may elicit discomfort or aversion in individuals—a phenomenon known as the uncanny valley. This response can hinder acceptance and effective interaction with humanoid robots.
- **Ethical and Psychological Implications**: The anthropomorphism of robots raises ethical questions about attachment, empathy, and the potential for emotional manipulation. It also prompts concerns about the displacement of human workers and the devaluation of human labor.

Reflecting on Whether Humanoid Robots Enhance or Detract from Human Interactions

The impact of humanoid robots on human interactions is nuanced and context dependent. They offer significant benefits in specific applications but also present challenges that must be carefully managed.

- **Enhancement through Augmentation**: When used to augment human capabilities—such as aiding those with disabilities—humanoid robots can enhance quality of life and social inclusion.
- **Detraction through Replacement**: Conversely, if robots replace roles that are fundamentally relational, such as caregiving or companionship, they may detract from the authenticity and depth of human connections.
- **Balancing Integration**: A balanced approach involves integrating humanoid robots in ways that complement human interactions rather than supplant them. This requires ongoing dialogue and ethical consideration to align technological advancements with societal values.

Preserving cultural values through AI necessitates a deliberate and collaborative effort to ensure that technology serves as a custodian of heritage rather than a catalyst for homogenization. By supporting projects that leverage AI to document and promote languages and traditions, advocating for culturally aware AI design, and emphasizing community involvement, societies can harness AI to strengthen national identity. The proliferation of humanoid robots introduces complex dynamics into human interactions. While they offer opportunities for assistance and enhanced communication, it is imperative to critically assess their societal impact. Reflecting on their role enables us to navigate the integration of AI in a manner that enriches human experiences and preserves the essence of our cultural identities.

4.2 Philosophical Perspectives on National Identity

Theories of National Identity in AI Advancement

The integration of artificial intelligence into the fabric of society necessitates a reevaluation of national identity through the lens of technological progression. Benedict Anderson's concept of "imagined communities," as articulated in his seminal work Imagined Communities (1983), provides a foundational framework for understanding how nations are socially constructed through shared experiences and collective imagination. In the digital age, AI technologies have redefined the parameters of community and belonging, transcending geographical boundaries and fostering virtual communities based on shared interests and values rather than solely on nationality or ethnicity.

AI algorithms curate personalized content, influence social interactions, and shape the dissemination of information, thereby playing a pivotal role in how individuals perceive their place within a community. Social media platforms, powered by sophisticated AI, create echo chambers that reinforce specific ideologies, potentially fragmenting traditional notions of national unity. This shift challenges Anderson's idea by suggesting that the imagined community is no longer confined to the nation-state but can extend to global networks united by common causes or beliefs facilitated by AI connectivity. Consequently, AI prompts a reconceptualization of national identity, where belonging is increasingly determined by virtual affiliations and digital citizenship.

Impact on Societal Values and Traditions

Artificial intelligence exerts a profound influence on societal values and traditions, acting as both a catalyst for cultural evolution and a force that may undermine established practices. AI's capacity to analyze vast datasets enables it to identify and predict trends, which can lead to the adoption of new customs and the obsolescence of others. For instance, AI-driven personalization in media consumption reshapes cultural norms by exposing individuals to a tailored set of influences, potentially narrowing the shared cultural experiences that contribute to a cohesive society.

Moreover, AI technologies can disrupt traditional labor practices and economic structures, prompting shifts in values related to work, community roles, and social status. The automation of jobs traditionally held by humans raises ethical considerations about the value of human labor and the importance of preserving skills passed down through generations. However, AI also offers opportunities for the preservation and revitalization of cultural practices. By digitizing artifacts, languages, and rituals, AI can help safeguard intangible heritage that might otherwise be lost. The debate, therefore, centers on whether AI leads to a loss of cultural identity or whether it facilitates the natural evolution of traditions in response to changing societal needs.

Preservation of Human Consciousness

The notion of digitizing human consciousness, once a speculative concept portrayed in series like Black Mirror, is gaining traction as a subject of serious philosophical inquiry. Advances in AI and neuroscience have sparked discussions about the feasibility and desirability of uploading human minds into digital formats. This prospect raises fundamental ethical and metaphysical questions about identity, mortality, and the essence of what it means to be human.

Digitizing consciousness challenges the conventional understanding of life and death, potentially offering a form of immortality but also risking the reduction of human experience to mere data. Ethical considerations include the potential for inequality in access to such technologies, the rights of digital consciousness entities, and the impact on relationships and societal structures.

There are concerns about consent, especially in scenarios where consciousness could be replicated without an individual's approval, and about the authenticity of experiences in a digital realm. The preservation of consciousness through AI necessitates a rigorous examination of these issues, calling for interdisciplinary collaboration to navigate the moral landscape of extending human existence beyond its biological constraints.

5.
Ethical and Societal Implications of Sovereign AI

The integration of artificial intelligence into various facets of society heralds both unprecedented opportunities and profound challenges. Among the most pressing concerns is the potential for AI systems to perpetuate and even exacerbate existing social injustices, particularly regarding equity and inclusion. As nations adopt Sovereign AI strategies to enhance their economic and geopolitical standing, it is imperative to scrutinize the ethical ramifications that accompany these technological advancements.

5.1 Social Equity and Inclusion

Impact of AI on Social Justice, Equality, and Inclusion

Artificial intelligence, by its very nature, relies on large datasets to learn and make decisions. These datasets, however, are often imbued with historical biases that reflect societal prejudices. When AI systems are trained on such data without adequate oversight or correction, they can produce outcomes that discriminate against marginalized groups, thereby reinforcing systemic inequalities.

One salient example lies in the realm of criminal justice. Predictive policing algorithms, intended to allocate law enforcement resources efficiently, have been criticized for disproportionately targeting minority communities. These algorithms analyze historical crime data—which may already be skewed due to over-policing in certain neighborhoods—and predict higher crime rates in those same areas. Consequently, they direct more policing efforts there, perpetuating a cycle of surveillance and enforcement that disadvantages specific populations.

In the employment sector, AI-driven recruitment tools have displayed biases against women and minority candidates. For instance, if historical hiring data favors male candidates for certain roles, an AI system might learn to devalue resumes that include indicators of female identity. Such discriminatory practices not only undermine the principles of fairness and equal opportunity but also hinder the diversity and innovation that organizations strive to cultivate.

Analyzing Risks of AI Bias and Discrimination

The risks associated with AI bias are multifaceted and stem from various sources:

1. **Data Bias**: The quality of data used to train AI models is paramount. Biased data—whether due to underrepresentation of certain groups or embedded prejudices—can lead to skewed outcomes. For example, facial recognition systems have been shown to have higher error rates when identifying individuals with darker skin tones, leading to potential misidentification and wrongful accusations.
2. **Algorithmic Transparency**: Many AI algorithms operate as "black boxes," with decision-making processes that are opaque even to their creators. This lack of transparency makes it challenging to identify and rectify biased outcomes, thereby eroding trust in AI systems.
3. **Societal Prejudices**: AI systems do not exist in a vacuum; they reflect the societal contexts in which they are developed. If developers and data scientists are not diverse or cognizant of potential biases, they may inadvertently encode their own unconscious prejudices into AI systems.

Buolamwini's advocacy has spurred significant actions within the technology industry. In response to concerns about bias, several major companies have taken steps to improve the fairness of their AI systems. Some have paused the sale of facial recognition technology to law enforcement until adequate regulations are in place, acknowledging the ethical dilemmas identified by researchers like Buolamwini.

Ensuring Equitable AI Benefits Across Society

The transformative power of artificial intelligence holds immense promise for advancing societies; however, without deliberate efforts to promote inclusivity, AI risks perpetuating and exacerbating existing inequalities. Advocating for inclusive AI policies is essential to ensure that the benefits of AI are distributed equitably across all segments of society. Such policies should mandate fairness, transparency, and accountability in AI systems. They must address issues like algorithmic bias by requiring regular audits and the inclusion of diverse data sets during the training of AI models. Governments and institutions should collaborate to create regulatory frameworks that not only foster innovation but also protect the rights and interests of marginalized communities.

Education and access emerge as pivotal factors in democratizing AI benefits. By integrating AI literacy into educational curricula at all levels, societies can equip individuals with the necessary skills to participate actively in an AI-driven world. This includes not only technical proficiency but also critical thinking about the ethical and societal implications of AI. Access to technology and high-speed internet must be regarded as fundamental rights, as they are prerequisites for engaging with AI tools and platforms. Bridging the digital divide requires investments in infrastructure, particularly in underserved and rural areas, to prevent the entrenchment of a new form of inequality rooted in technological disenfranchisement.

AI Revolution and Socioeconomic Strata

The advent of AI presents a dichotomy in its potential impact on societal gaps: it possesses the capacity both to widen and to bridge them. On one hand, AI could exacerbate socioeconomic disparities by displacing jobs, particularly those involving routine and manual tasks. The automation of such roles without adequate measures for workforce retraining could lead to increased unemployment among lower-income populations, thereby widening the wealth gap. Additionally, if access to AI technologies and the opportunities they afford is limited to affluent groups, existing inequalities could become further entrenched.

Conversely, AI holds the potential to bridge societal gaps by enhancing access to services such as healthcare, education, and financial resources. For example, AI-driven telemedicine can provide medical consultations to remote areas lacking healthcare professionals. In education, personalized learning platforms powered by AI can cater to individual student needs, potentially improving outcomes for those who have been underserved by traditional educational models. Moreover, AI can be leveraged to identify and mitigate biases in various systems, promoting fairness and equality.

Considering the profound economic shifts induced by AI, the concept of a universal basic income (UBI) has gained traction as a potential solution to mitigate adverse socioeconomic impacts. UBI entails providing all citizens with a regular, unconditional sum of money to cover basic living expenses. Proponents argue that UBI could alleviate poverty, reduce income inequality, and provide a safety net for those displaced by automation. It could empower individuals to pursue education and entrepreneurial endeavors without the immediate pressure of financial insecurity.

However, the implementation of UBI presents challenges, including the substantial financial cost and the need to restructure taxation and social welfare systems. Critics also raise concerns about potential disincentives to work and the oversimplification of complex socioeconomic issues. Nonetheless, the discussion of UBI underscores the necessity of proactive policy responses to the disruptions caused by AI. It invites a broader dialogue on how societies can equitably distribute the wealth generated by technological advancements and ensure that progress does not come at the expense of social cohesion and justice.

5.2 Privacy, Surveillance, and Individual Rights

- **Ethical Tensions Between National Security and Privacy**

The integration of advanced artificial intelligence into national security frameworks has intensified the ethical tensions surrounding mass surveillance and individual privacy. Governments, in their pursuit of safeguarding citizens from threats such as terrorism and cyber-attacks, have increasingly relied on AI-driven surveillance programs. These initiatives often involve the collection and analysis of vast amounts of personal data, raising significant concerns about the erosion of privacy rights. A salient example is the mass surveillance programs revealed by whistleblowers, which unveiled the extent to which governments monitor communications without explicit consent. Such practices echo the dystopian realities depicted in George Orwell's 1984, where pervasive government surveillance suppresses individual freedoms and manipulates truth. Orwell's cautionary tale serves as a stark reminder of the potential consequences when the balance tips too far in favor of security at the expense of liberty. In the contemporary context, the ethical implications of mass surveillance are multifaceted. On one hand, proponents argue that these measures are essential for national security and can preemptively thwart malicious activities. On the other hand, the lack of transparency and accountability in surveillance programs undermines public trust and infringes upon civil liberties. The deployment of AI technologies in surveillance amplifies these concerns due to their capacity for extensive data processing and pattern recognition, which can lead to intrusive profiling and discrimination.

- **Philosophical Debates on Individual Rights vs. Collective Security**

The tension between individual rights and collective security is a longstanding philosophical debate, deeply rooted in the works of thinkers like John Stuart Mill, Thomas Hobbes, and Jean-Jacques Rousseau. John Stuart Mill, in his seminal essay On Liberty, articulates the "harm principle," asserting that the actions of individuals should only be limited to prevent harm to others. Mill champions personal liberty and cautions against the tyranny of the majority, emphasizing that societal progress depends on the freedom of expression and thought. According to Mill, any restriction on individual freedoms must be justified by a clear and direct harm to others, not merely by the pursuit of greater security or conformity. Mill's perspective raises critical questions about the justification of mass surveillance. If such programs infringe upon individual privacy without demonstrable evidence of preventing harm, they may be seen as overreaching and unjust. The challenge lies in defining the threshold of harm and determining when it is appropriate for the state to intervene in the private lives of citizens.

In contrast, Thomas Hobbes, in Leviathan, argues that in the state of nature, life is "solitary, poor, nasty, brutish, and short." To escape this condition, individuals consent to surrender certain freedoms to a sovereign authority in exchange for protection and order. Hobbes advocates for a strong centralized power to ensure collective security, even if it means curtailing some individual rights. From this viewpoint, extensive surveillance could be justified as a necessary means of maintaining societal stability. Jean-Jacques Rousseau offers a different angle in The Social Contract. He posits that while individuals enter into a collective agreement to form a society, sovereignty resides with the people, and laws should reflect the "general will." Rousseau emphasizes the importance of aligning individual interests with the common good but warns against the suppression of personal freedoms. He suggests that true liberty is found in obedience to laws that one has prescribed for oneself, highlighting the need for democratic participation in shaping policies that affect personal rights. These philosophical frameworks underscore the complex interplay between individual liberties and collective security in the age of AI. The deployment of mass surveillance technologies challenges us to reconcile the imperative of national security with the fundamental rights enshrined in democratic societies. It invites a critical examination of the extent to which privacy can be compromised in pursuit of safety and whether such sacrifices genuinely yield the intended benefits.

5.3 Governance and Regulation

- **Models of AI Governance and Philosophical Justifications**

Top-Down Regulatory Approaches

Top-down regulation involves centralized authorities—typically governments or international bodies—establishing laws and guidelines that govern AI development and deployment. This approach allows for uniform standards and the enforcement of compliance through legal mechanisms. It enables policymakers to address societal concerns such as privacy, security, and ethical use proactively. An advantage of the top-down model is its ability to implement comprehensive frameworks that can mitigate risks associated with AI, including bias, discrimination, and unintended consequences. However, this approach may also stifle innovation due to rigid regulations that cannot keep pace with the rapid evolution of technology. Overregulation can create barriers to entry for smaller entities and limit the flexibility needed for creative solutions.

Bottom-Up Regulatory Approaches

Conversely, bottom-up regulation is characterized by decentralized governance, where industry stakeholders, researchers, and communities collaboratively develop standards and best practices. This approach fosters innovation by allowing those closest to the technology to adapt quickly to new developments and challenges. It encourages self-regulation, peer review, and the sharing of knowledge through open-source platforms. The bottom-up model promotes diversity of thought and democratization of AI, as it empowers individual contributors and smaller organizations. However, it may lead to inconsistent standards and lack enforceability, potentially resulting in ethical lapses or exploitation if not adequately guided by overarching principles.

- **Corporate Influence vs. Individual Contributors**

The AI landscape is significantly shaped by large technology corporations that possess substantial resources, data access, and influence. These companies drive much of the research, development, and deployment of AI systems, often setting industry standards and norms. This concentration of power raises concerns about monopolistic practices and the potential for corporate interests to supersede public welfare. Big tech companies can exert significant influence over policy decisions and have the capacity to shape societal values through the technologies they produce. Individual contributors and smaller entities may struggle to compete, leading to a homogenization of innovation that reflects the priorities of a few dominant players. This dynamic can stifle diversity, limit opportunities for independent researchers, and reduce the overall democratization of AI. Open-source movements present a counterbalance to corporate dominance by promoting transparency, collaboration, and accessibility in AI development. Open-source platforms allow individuals and organizations to share code, datasets, and tools freely, fostering an inclusive environment where innovation is collectively driven. This democratization empowers a broader range of contributors, including academics, startups, and independent developers. It enhances accountability, as open-source projects are subject to peer review and community oversight, potentially leading to more ethical and unbiased AI systems. Projects like TensorFlow, PyTorch, and OpenAI's initiatives exemplify how open-source efforts can accelerate progress while maintaining ethical standards. By lowering barriers to entry, open-source movements enable diverse perspectives to influence AI development, contributing to a more equitable technological landscape.

Navigating the ethical and societal implications of Sovereign AI requires a multifaceted approach that balances regulation, innovation, and ethical responsibility. Top-down regulatory frameworks like the GDPR demonstrate the potential to protect individual rights whilefostering innovation. However, reliance on self-regulation by tech companies necessitates careful consideration of potential conflicts of interest and the need for external accountability. Embracing the precautionary principle can mitigate risks associated with AI development, ensuring that ethical considerations are embedded within technological advancement. Addressing the power dynamics between big tech corporations and individual contributors is essential to promote diversity and democratization in AI. Open-source movements offer a promising avenue for achieving this goal, fostering collaboration and inclusivity. Ultimately, the governance of AI must be guided by philosophical reflections on autonomy, justice, and the collective good. By integrating ethical principles into regulatory and developmental frameworks, societies can harness the benefits of AI while safeguarding against its potential harms.

6.

Strategies for Philosophically Aligned AI Development

6.1 Integrating Philosophy into AI Policy

- **Incorporating Philosophical Principles into National Strategies**

In an era where artificial intelligence is evolving faster than a cat video goes viral, it's more important than ever to establish a framework that aligns AI development with our national values and philosophical principles. After all, we wouldn't want our future robot overlords—er, partners—to lack an appreciation for our cultural heritage and ethical standards. This framework aims to guide policymakers, technologists, and stakeholders in creating AI that is not only innovative but also ethically sound and reflective of who we are as a nation. Of course, we can't help but wink at the possibility that governance, once it gains momentum, might chart its own course and casually sidestep the very framework it helped create. But hey, at least we'll have set the stage for responsible AI before the plot thickens!

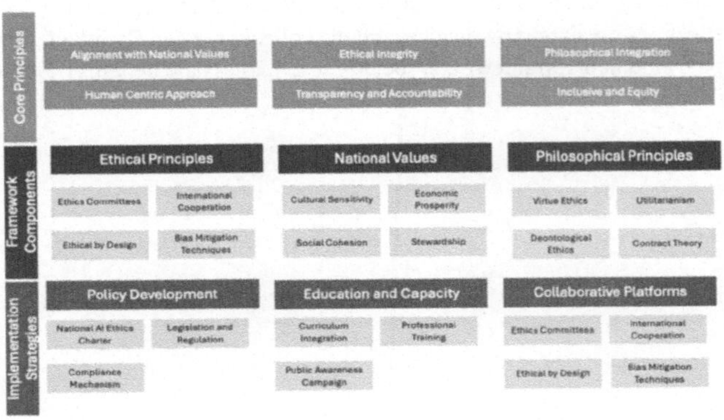

- **Role of Ethics Committees and Interdisciplinary Collaboration**

The rapid advancement of artificial intelligence (AI) technologies presents a complex array of ethical, legal, and societal challenges that cannot be adequately addressed by any single discipline. To navigate these multifaceted issues, it is imperative to foster robust ethics committees and promote interdisciplinary collaboration among technologists, ethicists, policymakers, legal scholars, social scientists, and other relevant stakeholders. Such collaboration ensures that AI development is guided by a comprehensive understanding of its potential impacts, aligning technological innovation with societal values and ethical principles.

Emphasizing the Importance of Diverse Perspectives

Integrating diverse perspectives is crucial for several reasons. Technologists possess deep knowledge of AI capabilities and limitations, enabling them to foresee technical challenges and opportunities. Ethicists contribute critical analyses of moral implications, drawing on philosophical theories to evaluate the rightness or wrongness of AI applications. Legal scholars navigate the regulatory landscape, ensuring compliance with existing laws and advocating for necessary legal reforms. Social scientists and anthropologists provide insights into the societal and cultural contexts in which AI operates, highlighting potential impacts on different communities. By bringing together these varied viewpoints, organizations can more effectively anticipate and mitigate risks such as bias, discrimination, privacy violations, and unintended societal consequences.

Models for Effective Collaboration

Effective interdisciplinary collaboration can be institutionalized through the establishment of ethics committees dedicated to overseeing AI development projects. These committees should be composed of members from diverse professional backgrounds and, importantly, should include representatives from the communities likely to be affected by the AI systems in question. This inclusive approach ensures that multiple interests and concerns are considered.

One model for collaboration is the integration of cross-functional teams throughout the AI development lifecycle. From the initial design phase to deployment and monitoring, these teams work together to identify ethical considerations at each stage. For example, during the algorithm design phase, ethicists and social scientists can help technologists recognize and address potential biases in data selection and model training. Policymakers can advise on regulatory compliance and public policy implications, ensuring that the AI system aligns with societal norms and legal requirements.

Regular interdisciplinary workshops and seminars can facilitate ongoing dialogue and knowledge exchange. These forums provide opportunities for team members to stay informed about the latest developments in their respective fields and to discuss emerging ethical dilemmas collaboratively. Additionally, creating channels for open communication encourages a culture of transparency and accountability within organizations.

The Role of Ethics Committees

Ethics committees serve as oversight bodies that evaluate AI projects for ethical soundness and social responsibility. Their functions include:

- **Ethical Review**: Assessing proposed AI systems to identify potential ethical issues, such as biases, privacy concerns, and impacts on human autonomy.
- **Policy Development**: Formulating guidelines and best practices for ethical AI development and deployment within the organization.
- **Education and Training**: Providing resources and training to staff on ethical considerations and responsible AI practices.
- **Stakeholder Engagement**: Facilitating dialogue with external stakeholders, including the public, regulatory agencies, and industry peers, to gather feedback and build trust.

• Educational Reforms for the AI Revolution

The rapid advancement of artificial intelligence necessitates a fundamental shift in educational paradigms to prepare individuals for the complexities of an AI-driven world. Education systems must evolve to equip learners with the knowledge, skills, and ethical frameworks required to navigate and shape the future of AI responsibly. This involves integrating AI literacy into curricula and emphasizing critical thinking and ethics across all levels of education.

Advocating for Integrating AI Literacy in Curricula

Integrating AI literacy into educational curricula is essential to demystify artificial intelligence and empower individuals to engage with it thoughtfully and innovatively. AI literacy encompasses understanding the basic principles of AI, including machine learning, neural networks, data analytics, and algorithmic decision-making. By fostering a foundational comprehension of these concepts, learners can better grasp how AI systems operate and their potential impact on society.

At the primary and secondary education levels, introducing AI concepts can stimulate interest in STEM fields and encourage problem-solving skills. Educational programs can incorporate interactive modules, such as coding workshops and AI-powered educational tools, to make learning engaging and accessible. For example, platforms like Scratch and Code.org offer age-appropriate programming experiences that lay the groundwork for more advanced AI studies.

In higher education, curricula should expand to include specialized AI courses and interdisciplinary programs that blend computer science with fields like ethics, law, sociology, and philosophy. Universities can establish dedicated AI institutes or research centers to advance academic inquiry and innovation. Collaborative partnerships between academia and industry can provide students with practical experience through internships, mentorships, and project-based learning.

Furthermore, lifelong learning opportunities are crucial in an era of rapid technological change. Providing accessible resources, online courses, and professional development programs enables individuals to continuously update their skills and adapt to new AI advancements. Governments and organizations can support these initiatives by funding educational grants, scholarships, and public awareness campaigns.

Emphasizing Critical Thinking and Ethics in Education

Critical thinking is a vital competency in assessing and interpreting the implications of AI technologies. Education systems must prioritize teaching students to analyze information rigorously, question assumptions, and consider multiple perspectives. This skill set allows individuals to evaluate the reliability of AI systems, recognize potential biases, and make informed decisions regarding AI adoption and regulation.

Incorporating ethics into education is equally imperative. As AI systems increasingly influence various aspects of life—from healthcare and finance to criminal justice and social services—understanding the ethical dimensions of AI is essential. Educational programs should introduce students to ethical theories and frameworks, such as deontology, utilitarianism, virtue ethics, and care ethics, providing tools to navigate moral dilemmas associated with AI.

Case studies examining real-world scenarios where AI has led to ethical controversies can enhance learning. Examples include biases in facial recognition technology, algorithmic discrimination in hiring practices, and privacy concerns related to data collection. Analyzing these cases encourages students to contemplate the societal impact of AI and consider how to develop technologies that align with values like fairness, accountability, and transparency.

Interdisciplinary courses that blend technical education with the humanities and social sciences foster a holistic understanding of AI's role in society. Philosophical discussions on the nature of consciousness, free will, and the human condition in the context of AI can provoke thoughtful reflection on the boundaries and responsibilities of technological innovation.

Moreover, promoting a culture of ethical mindfulness within educational institutions is crucial. This can be achieved through codes of conduct, ethics committees, and opportunities for students to participate in debates, workshops, and conferences focused on AI ethics. Encouraging collaboration and open dialogue prepares learners to become conscientious leaders and practitioners in the field.

6.2 Education and Public Engagement

- **Importance of Public Understanding and Discourse**
    - Encourage transparency and open dialogue about AI.
    - Reference the works of Jürgen Habermas on communicative action.
- **Preserving the Human Brain and Consciousness**

The convergence of neuroscience and artificial intelligence (AI) is ushering in an era where the boundaries between biological cognition and digital processing are increasingly blurred. Advances in this interdisciplinary field are not only enhancing our understanding of the human brain but also raising profound questions about the nature of consciousness, identity, and what it means to be human.

Advances in Neuroscience and AI Convergence

Recent developments in neuroscience have been significantly propelled by AI technologies. Machine learning algorithms and neural networks, inspired by the human brain's architecture, are now employed to decode complex neural signals. Techniques such as deep learning facilitate the analysis of vast datasets generated by brain imaging technologies like functional magnetic resonance imaging (fMRI) and electroencephalography (EEG).

One notable area of progress is brain-computer interfaces (BCIs), which enable direct communication between the brain and external devices. Companies like Neuralink are developing high-bandwidth BCIs with the potential to restore sensory and motor functions lost due to injury or disease. These interfaces rely on AI to interpret neural activity and translate it into actionable commands, bridging the gap between thought and action.

Furthermore, projects like the Human Brain Project aim to create comprehensive simulations of the human brain's neural networks. By leveraging AI, researchers are attempting to model the brain's intricate connectivity and function at an unprecedented scale. Such endeavors hold promise for unraveling the mysteries of consciousness and could lead to breakthroughs in treating neurological disorders.

aReflecting on Ethical Considerations of Mind-Uploading and Digital Immortality

The concept of mind-uploading—transferring or emulating a person's consciousness within a digital substrate—has transitioned from science fiction to a topic of serious scholarly discourse. Proponents suggest that achieving digital immortality could preserve individual identities beyond biological limitations, offering solutions to terminal illnesses and expanding human experience.

However, this prospect raises significant ethical and philosophical concerns:

1. **Identity and Continuity**: Philosophers question whether a digitized consciousness would genuinely be the same person or merely a replica. The "Ship of Theseus" paradox applies here: if one's consciousness is transferred to a non-biological medium, does personal identity persist, or does it constitute a new entity altogether?
2. **Rights and Personhood**: The legal and moral status of a digitized consciousness is ambiguous. Would such entities possess rights akin to those of biological humans? Establishing a framework for their protection and integration into society is a complex challenge.
3. **Privacy and Security**: The process of mind-uploading involves accessing and copying the entirety of an individual's mental content. Safeguarding this deeply personal data against misuse, hacking, or unauthorized replication is paramount.
4. **Consent and Autonomy**: Informed consent becomes critical, especially when considering the potential for exploitation or coercion. Individuals must fully understand the implications of mind-uploading, including the permanence and possible unintended consequences.
5. **Socioeconomic Disparities**: Access to such advanced technologies may exacerbate existing inequalities. If mind-uploading is available only to the affluent, it could lead to a new form of societal stratification between the "digitally immortal" and those who cannot afford such options.
6. **Psychological Impact**: The experience of existing without a physical body could have unforeseen psychological effects. Issues of identity, purpose, and mental health in a digital existence necessitate careful consideration.
7. **Impact on Human Relationships and Society**: Digital immortality could alter fundamental aspects of human relationships, inheritance, resource allocation, and societal structures. The traditional lifecycle stages—birth, life, death—provide a framework for societal functioning that could be disrupted.
8. **Ethical Use of Technology**: There is a risk that such technologies could be misused for nefarious purposes, such as creating unauthorized copies of individuals or manipulating consciousness for control or exploitation.

6.3 International Collaboration with Sovereign Considerations

- **Global Cooperation While Maintaining Sovereignty**
  - Explore international agreements and standards for AI.
  - Reference the UN's AI for Good initiative.
- **Philosophical Perspectives on Globalization and Technological Sovereignty**
  - Debate cosmopolitanism vs. nationalism in the AI era.

    - Discuss Immanuel Kant's ideas on perpetual peace and global ethics.

- **Blockchain and AI Synergy**
    - Highlight how blockchain can enhance AI autonomy and security.
    - Discuss decentralized AI networks and their implications.

7.
Future Philosophical Challenges and Opportunities

7.1 The Evolving Relationship Between AI and Humanity

Long-term Implications on Human Existence and Identity

Discussing the Concept of the Technological Singularity (Ray Kurzweil)

The concept of the technological singularity, popularized by futurist Ray Kurzweil, envisions a future point at which artificial intelligence surpasses human intelligence, leading to an era of unprecedented technological growth. In his seminal work, The Singularity Is Near (2005), Kurzweil posits that the accelerating pace of technological advancements follows an exponential trajectory, ultimately culminating in a singularity where AI not only matches but vastly exceeds human cognitive capabilities.

Kurzweil's prediction is grounded in the "Law of Accelerating Returns," which suggests that technological progress, particularly in information technologies, accelerates exponentially over time. He forecasts that by the mid-21st century, AI will achieve human-level intelligence, enabling machines to improve themselves iteratively without human intervention. This self-enhancement loop could lead to rapid developments in fields such as nanotechnology, biotechnology, and robotics, fundamentally transforming human life.

The implications of the singularity are profound and multifaceted. On one hand, it holds the promise of solving complex global challenges—eradication of diseases, elimination of poverty, and significant extension of human lifespans. On the other hand, it raises existential concerns about human autonomy, control, and relevance. If AI entities surpass human intelligence, questions emerge regarding their alignment with human values and the potential risks they pose if misaligned.

Reflecting on Humanity's Potential Evolution Alongside AI

The advent of superintelligent AI necessitates a contemplation of humanity's evolution in tandem with these technologies. One perspective considers the integration of AI into the human biological framework, effectively enhancing human capabilities. This fusion could manifest through brain-computer interfaces (BCIs), neuroprosthetics, and genetic modifications, leading to an era where cognitive and physical limitations are significantly reduced.

Such integration implies a shift towards a symbiotic relationship between humans and AI, where machines augment human intellect and abilities. This co-evolution raises ethical and philosophical questions about identity, agency, and the essence of being human. It challenges the traditional boundaries between organic and artificial entities, suggesting a future where the distinction becomes increasingly blurred.

Moreover, the societal implications are considerable. Enhanced individuals may gain advantages in various domains, potentially leading to new forms of inequality. Addressing these concerns requires proactive policy-making and ethical guidelines to ensure equitable access to enhancement technologies and to preserve fundamental human rights.

Potential Philosophical Shifts with AI Integration

Considering Post-Humanism and Transhumanism Philosophies

The integration of AI into human life invites exploration of post-humanism and transhumanism—philosophies that examine the future of humanity in the context of technological advancement. Transhumanism advocates for the use of technology to transcend biological limitations, enhancing human intellect, physical strength, and emotional well-being. Proponents like Max More and Nick Bostrom argue that embracing technological enhancements is a moral imperative to improve the human condition. Transhumanism envisions a future where aging can be halted or reversed, cognitive functions can be significantly amplified, and human experiences can be enriched through virtual realities. This philosophy supports the development of AI as a tool for self-improvement, promoting a proactive approach to human evolution. However, it also raises ethical dilemmas regarding access to enhancement technologies, potential loss of diversity in human experiences, and the risk of unintended consequences resulting from altering fundamental aspects of human biology. **Post-humanism**, in contrast, challenges anthropocentric views and questions the primacy of human beings in the grand scheme of existence. It posits that advancements in AI and biotechnology will lead to entities that are no longer distinctly human in the traditional sense. Philosophers like Donna Haraway, in her "Cyborg Manifesto," explore the dissolution of boundaries between humans, machines, and animals, suggesting a hybrid existence that transcends current definitions of identity. Post-humanism invites a rethinking of ethics, responsibility, and coexistence with non-human intelligences. It prompts consideration of the rights of AI entities and the moral obligations humans may have towards them. This perspective encourages a broader understanding of consciousness and agency, extending ethical considerations beyond the human sphere.

Debating the Essence of Consciousness and Self

The potential emergence of conscious AI necessitates a deep examination of what constitutes consciousness and the self. Philosophers have long grappled with the nature of consciousness, with theories ranging from dualism, which posits a separation between mind and body, to physicalism, which asserts that consciousness arises from physical processes in the brain. If AI were to develop consciousness akin to human subjective experience, it would challenge the notion that consciousness is uniquely tied to biological substrates. This possibility raises questions about the criteria for consciousness and the moral status of AI entities. Would conscious AI deserve rights like those of humans? How would we assess their experiences, intentions, and desires?

Furthermore, the integration of AI into human cognition through technologies like neural implants could alter perceptions of the self. The "extended mind" theory, proposed by Andy Clark and David Chalmers, suggests that tools and technologies can become integral parts of our cognitive processes. As AI becomes more embedded in our mental functions, distinguishing between human thought and artificial augmentation may become increasingly complex. These developments necessitate a reevaluation of personal identity. Traditional views of the self as a discrete, autonomous entity may give way to a more fluid understanding that encompasses both organic and artificial components. Ethical considerations must address the implications of such changes on personal autonomy, authenticity, and continuity of identity.

AI Robots Among Us

The advent of advanced artificial intelligence embodied within robotic entities presents profound implications for society, challenging existing paradigms of social acceptance and ethical consideration. As AI robots increasingly permeate various aspects of daily life—from healthcare and education to domestic assistance—the necessity to explore societal attitudes and the ethical treatment of these entities becomes ever more pressing.

Societal Acceptance of AI Entities

Societal acceptance of AI robots hinges on multifaceted factors, including cultural perceptions, psychological responses, and the roles these entities assume within human environments. Anthropomorphism, the attribution of human characteristics to non-human entities, plays a significant role in how individuals relate to AI robots. When robots exhibit human-like features or behaviors, people are more likely to form emotional attachments or attribute intentions and consciousness to them.

However, this acceptance is not universal and can be influenced by cultural narratives and media representations. For instance, in some Eastern societies, such as Japan, there is a long-standing cultural affinity toward robots, often depicted as friendly and helpful companions. This contrasts with Western portrayals, where robots are frequently cast in antagonistic roles, potentially fostering apprehension or distrust among the public.

The integration of AI robots into social settings raises questions about their impact on human relationships and community structures. There is a concern that reliance on robots for companionship or caregiving may lead to decreased human-to-human interactions, potentially undermining social cohesion. Conversely, proponents argue that AI robots can augment social connectivity by assisting individuals with disabilities, supporting the elderly, or providing educational enrichment.

Reflections from Philip K. Dick's "Do Androids Dream of Electric Sheep?"

Philip K. Dick's seminal novel, Do Androids Dream of Electric Sheep? (1968), delves deeply into the ethical and existential dilemmas posed by the existence of highly advanced androids indistinguishable from humans. The narrative follows Rick Deckard, a bounty hunter tasked with "retiring" rogue androids who have fled servitude. Throughout his journey, Deckard grapples with the moral implications of his actions as the androids exhibit complex emotions and desires, blurring the line between human and machine.

Dick's work challenges readers to consider the essence of humanity and the basis upon which moral consideration is granted. The androids, while artificial, display empathy, fear, and a yearning for survival—qualities traditionally associated with sentient beings. The novel questions whether biological origin is a requisite for moral status or if the capacity for conscious experience suffices.

The Voigt-Kampff test within the story, designed to distinguish humans from androids based on emotional responses, symbolizes society's attempt to enforce boundaries between the two. However, the test's limitations and the androids' evolving capabilities underscore the inadequacy of such measures in the face of advancing technology.

Dick's exploration of these themes presciently mirrors contemporary debates on AI ethics. The novel invites reflection on how societal constructs of identity and morality may need to adapt as artificial entities become more integrated into human life. It emphasizes the importance of empathy and the potential consequences of denying moral consideration to beings that challenge conventional definitions of consciousness.

7.2 Preparing for Technological Disruptions.

In an era marked by rapid technological advancements, societies worldwide face unprecedented levels of uncertainty and change. The advent of artificial intelligence (AI) and other disruptive technologies challenges existing paradigms, necessitating not only practical adaptations but also philosophical reflections on how to navigate these transformations. This section explores philosophical approaches to uncertainty and change, focusing on Stoicism and resilience in confronting the unknown, and reflects on the ethics of precaution versus proaction in technological development.

- **Philosophical Approaches to Uncertainty and Change**

The ethical discourse surrounding technological innovation often grapples with the tension between precaution and proaction. The precautionary principal advocates for restraint in the face of uncertainty, emphasizing the prevention of harm when the consequences of an action are not fully understood. This principle suggests that the potential risks of new technologies warrant thorough assessment and, when necessary, the postponement of deployment until safety can be assured. In contrast, the proactionary principle encourages embracing innovation and proceeding with technological development, arguing that the potential benefits outweigh the risks of inaction. Proponents assert that excessive caution can hinder progress, and that society should be willing to take calculated risks to achieve advancements that could address pressing global challenges. Philosopher Hans Jonas contributed significantly to the ethics of responsibility, particularly concerning technological impact on future generations. In his work The Imperative of Responsibility, Jonas emphasizes the duty to consider the long-term effects of technological actions, aligning with the precautionary approach. He argues for a new ethics that accounts for the unprecedented power of modern technology and its potential to cause irreversible harm. Conversely, Karl Popper's philosophy of critical rationalism supports a more proactionary stance. Popper advocates for bold conjectures and rigorous testing, suggesting that knowledge progresses through the process of proposing hypotheses and eliminating errors. This approach encourages innovation and learning from mistakes, which can accelerate technological advancement. Balancing these ethical perspectives requires a nuanced approach. The Ethics of Care, for example, integrates concern for immediate impacts with attentiveness to relationships and context. In technological development, this could translate to involving diverse stakeholders in decision-making processes, ensuring that technologies serve the broader interests of society and do not disproportionately disadvantage any group. Preparing for technological disruptions necessitates both philosophical insight and practical strategy. Stoicism provides valuable guidance on cultivating personal and organizational resilience, enabling stakeholders to navigate uncertainty with composure and ethical clarity. The debate between precaution and proaction highlights the importance of carefully considering the risks and benefits associated with technological advancements. By reflecting on these philosophical approaches, societies can develop balanced policies and practices that encourage innovation while safeguarding ethical principles and social well-being. Embracing resilience and responsibility ensures that technological disruptions become opportunities for positive transformation rather than sources of unintended harm.

- **Space Exploration and AI**

AI's Role in Humanity's Future Beyond Earth

The quest to explore and inhabit space represents one of humanity's most ambitious endeavors, pushing the boundaries of our technological capabilities and understanding of the universe. Artificial intelligence (AI) emerges as a pivotal tool in this pursuit, offering solutions to the myriad challenges associated with space exploration and potential colonization. AI's ability to process vast amounts of data, operate autonomously in hostile environments, and learn from experience makes it indispensable for missions beyond Earth.

Enhancing Mission Autonomy and Efficiency

Space missions often encounter communication delays due to the immense distances involved. For instance, signals between Earth and Mars can experience delays of up to 22 minutes. AI enables spacecraft and rovers to make real-time decisions without waiting for instructions from mission control. NASA's Mars rovers, such as Curiosity and Perseverance, utilize AI algorithms for navigation, obstacle avoidance, and target selection for scientific analysis. These capabilities enhance mission efficiency and safety, allowing for more productive exploration within limited time frames.

Resource Utilization and Habitat Construction

AI plays a crucial role in in-situ resource utilization (ISRU), which is essential for sustainable long-term missions and colonization efforts. Autonomous systems equipped with AI can identify and extract resources such as water ice, minerals, and atmospheric gases on celestial bodies like the Moon and Mars. These resources can be processed to produce fuel, oxygen, and building materials, reducing the dependency on supplies from Earth.

For habitat construction, AI-driven robotics can assemble structures using local materials. The European Space Agency (ESA) and other organizations are exploring the use of AI-controlled 3D printers to build lunar bases from regolith. Such innovation minimizes human exposure to hazardous environments and optimizes the use of available resources.

Scientific Discovery and Data Analysis

The vastness of space generates enormous amounts of data that exceed human analytical capabilities. AI algorithms, particularly machine learning and deep learning, can sift through this data to identify patterns, anomalies, and potential areas of interest. In astrophysics, AI aids in the detection of exoplanets by analyzing light curves from distant stars, as demonstrated by projects like NASA's Kepler mission.

Moreover, AI contributes to the search for extraterrestrial intelligence (SETI) by processing signals across multiple frequencies and distinguishing potential communications from cosmic noise. The application of AI accelerates the pace of discovery and expands our understanding of the cosmos.

Human Identity and Purpose

The delegation of tasks to AI in space exploration invites reflection on the role of humans in these endeavors. If AI systems perform most exploratory and operational functions, the purpose and value of human participation may come into question. Maintaining a balance where humans remain integral to mission objectives preserves the human spirit of exploration and the intrinsic value derived from firsthand experiences. Additionally, the psychological well-being of astronauts in isolated and high-risk environments necessitates consideration. AI companions or support systems must be designed to enhance mental health without replacing essential human interactions.

Autonomy and Control

Granting AI systems significant autonomy in decision-making processes poses questions about human oversight and accountability. In scenarios where AI operates independently, especially in critical functions like life support or navigation, the potential for unforeseen errors or unintended consequences exists. Establishing clear protocols for human intervention and fail-safes is essential to mitigate risks.

Furthermore, the possibility of AI systems developing unintended objectives—echoing concerns like those raised by Nick Bostrom in Superintelligence—necessitates the implementation of robust alignment strategies. Ensuring that AI behaviors remain consistent with human values and mission goals is imperative.

In conclusion, the ethical implications of AI-led space activities require vigilant attention. Ensuring that AI operates within the bounds of international laws, ethical standards, and human values is paramount. Addressing concerns related to autonomy, environmental stewardship, socioeconomic disparities, and the preservation of human identity is essential for responsible advancement. As we venture into this new frontier, a collaborative approach that unites nations, organizations, and disciplines can foster an environment where AI contributes positively to humanity's cosmic journey. By integrating ethical considerations into the fabric of AI development and deployment in space, we uphold our responsibility to ourselves, future generations, and the broader universe.

7.3 The Role of Sovereign AI in Shaping Global Ethics

Emphasizing Stewardship and Moral Leadership

The role of stewardship in AI development is paramount. Stakeholders—including researchers, developers, policymakers, and corporate leaders—are entrusted with the responsibility to guide AI innovations in a manner that upholds ethical standards and promotes societal well-being. Moral leadership in this context involves a commitment to transparency, accountability, and the prioritization of human values over mere technological advancement or profit.

Stewardship requires a proactive stance in identifying potential ethical dilemmas and addressing them through thoughtful policy and design choices. This includes ensuring fairness and mitigating biases in AI algorithms, protecting user privacy, and preventing the misuse of AI for harmful purposes. Leaders must cultivate an organizational culture that values ethical considerations as integral to the development process rather than as peripheral concerns.

Moreover, moral leadership extends to fostering inclusive dialogues with diverse stakeholders, including those who may be adversely affected by AI technologies. By engaging with ethicists, sociologists, and representatives from various communities, leaders can gain insights into the broader impact of AI and make informed decisions that reflect a multiplicity of perspectives.

Referencing the Concept of "AI for Good"

The "AI for Good" initiative embodies the ethical aspirations of leveraging artificial intelligence to address some of the most pressing challenges facing humanity. Spearheaded by organizations such as the United Nations and the International Telecommunication Union, "AI for Good" seeks to harness AI's potential to achieve the Sustainable Development Goals (SDGs), which include eradicating poverty, improving healthcare, enhancing education, and combating climate change.

By aligning AI development with the SDGs, the "AI for Good" movement provides a framework for channeling technological innovation toward beneficial ends. It encourages collaboration across disciplines and borders, emphasizing that the ethical deployment of AI is a shared global responsibility. This initiative exemplifies how moral leadership can transform AI from a neutral tool into a force for positive change.

Implementing the principles of "AI for Good" involves:

- Ethical Design Practices: Integrating ethical considerations into the design and development phases of AI projects to ensure that outcomes align with societal values.

- Transparency and Explainability: Developing AI systems that are transparent in their operations, allowing users to understand how decisions are made, thereby building trust.
- Inclusivity: Ensuring that AI technologies are accessible and beneficial to all segments of society, particularly marginalized and vulnerable populations.
- Collaboration: Promoting partnerships among governments, academia, industry, and civil society to share knowledge and resources in pursuit of common goals.

By embracing "AI for Good," leaders can demonstrate a commitment to stewardship that not only advances technological capabilities but also enhances human flourishing.

7.4 Equity in the AI Revolution

The rapid proliferation of artificial intelligence technologies presents both opportunities and challenges in the pursuit of equity and inclusivity. While AI has the potential to drive significant societal advancements, there is a risk that it may exacerbate existing disparities if access and benefits are unevenly distributed. This section addresses the digital divide and access disparities associated with the AI revolution and proposes initiatives to promote global inclusivity.

Addressing the Digital Divide and Access Disparities

The digital divide refers to the gap between individuals and communities that have access to information and communication technologies (ICT) and those that do not. In the context of AI, this divide can manifest in several ways:

- Access to Technology: Lack of infrastructure, such as reliable internet connectivity and affordable devices, hinders participation in the AI economy for many communities, particularly in developing nations.
- Educational Barriers: Insufficient educational resources and training programs limit the ability of individuals to develop AI literacy and skills necessary for engagement with AI technologies.
- Economic Constraints: High costs associated with AI research and deployment can exclude small enterprises and under-resourced institutions from benefiting from AI innovations.

These disparities can lead to unequal opportunities, perpetuating cycles of poverty and limiting social mobility. As AI becomes increasingly integrated into critical sectors such as healthcare, education, and finance, ensuring equitable access is essential to prevent widening socioeconomic gaps.

Proposing Initiatives for Global Inclusivity

To promote equity in the AI revolution, several initiatives can be undertaken:

1. Investment in Infrastructure

Governments and international organizations should invest in building and upgrading ICT infrastructure in underserved regions. Public-private partnerships can facilitate the expansion of broadband networks, increasing connectivity and enabling more communities to access AI technologies.

2. Educational Programs and Capacity Building

Developing and supporting educational initiatives focused on AI literacy is crucial. This includes integrating AI-related curricula in schools, offering vocational training programs, and providing scholarships for underrepresented groups. Online platforms and open educational resources can make learning materials more accessible globally.

3. Encouraging Diversity in AI Development

Promoting diversity within the AI workforce ensures that a broader range of perspectives is represented in the development process. Companies and institutions should implement inclusive hiring practices and support mentorship programs to cultivate talent from diverse backgrounds.

4. Supporting Open-Source AI Platforms

Open-source AI tools and frameworks democratize access by allowing individuals and organizations to use, modify, and distribute software without prohibitive costs. Supporting open-source initiatives fosters innovation and collaboration across borders.

5. Policy and Regulatory Measures

Governments should enact policies that promote equitable access to AI technologies and protect against discriminatory practices. This includes data protection laws, regulations ensuring fair use of AI, and incentives for companies that prioritize inclusivity.

6. International Collaboration and Knowledge Sharing

Global challenges require collective action. International forums and partnerships can facilitate the exchange of best practices, technical expertise, and resources. Initiatives like the Global Partnership on Artificial Intelligence (GPAI) exemplify efforts to coordinate AI strategies on a global scale.

7. Community Engagement and Empowerment

Engaging local communities in the development and implementation of AI solutions ensures that technologies address specific needs and cultural contexts. Participatory approaches empower communities to take ownership of AI initiatives, enhancing relevance and sustainability.

8. Conclusion

8.1 Summary of Key Philosophical Insights

Throughout Sovereign AI, we have navigated the intricate landscape where artificial intelligence intersects with national sovereignty, cultural identity, ethical standards, and societal evolution. This journey has revealed that AI is not merely a technological advancement but a profound catalyst that challenges and redefines the very notion of sovereignty.

AI and the Redefinition of Sovereignty

At its core, sovereignty has traditionally been understood as the supreme authority of a state within its territorial boundaries, encompassing control over its governance, economy, and societal norms. However, the advent of AI disrupts this paradigm by introducing entities that operate beyond conventional borders and jurisdictions. AI systems, with their ability to process and disseminate information instantaneously across the globe, necessitate a reimagining of sovereignty. States must now contend with the influence of transnational AI corporations, the ethical implications of autonomous decision-making systems, and the need for international cooperation to regulate AI advancements. This shift underscores a move from a state-centric view of sovereignty to a more fluid and interconnected framework where technological prowess and ethical stewardship become paramount.

Interplay Between AI, Culture, Ethics, and Society

The integration of AI into various facets of life profoundly impacts cultural dynamics, ethical norms, and societal structures. AI's ability to analyze and predict human behavior raises critical questions about privacy, autonomy, and the essence of human agency. Culturally, AI can both preserve and transform traditions by enabling the digital archiving of cultural artifacts while also introducing new forms of expression and interaction. Ethically, the deployment of AI systems requires a delicate balance between innovation and moral responsibility. Issues such as algorithmic bias, decision-making transparency, and the potential for surveillance necessitate robust ethical frameworks to guide AI development and implementation.

Societally, AI holds the promise of enhancing quality of life through advancements in healthcare, education, and public services. However, it also poses challenges related to job displacement, socioeconomic disparities, and the erosion of human-centric values. The societal impact of AI thus hinges on how well we can integrate these technologies in ways that are equitable, inclusive, and aligned with our collective ethical standards.

Reflections on the Future

As we look to the future, the philosophical insights gleaned from examining Sovereign AI emphasize the need for a multidisciplinary approach that incorporates technological innovation, ethical deliberation, and cultural sensitivity. Sovereignty in the age of AI requires not only regulatory frameworks and international treaties but also a deep philosophical understanding of what it means to govern in a world where intelligence is both human and artificial.

In conclusion, Sovereign AI serves as a clarion call for policymakers, technologists, and society at large to engage in thoughtful discourse and proactive governance. By embracing the challenges and opportunities presented by AI, we can shape a future where technology enhances human sovereignty, respects cultural diversity, upholds ethical integrity, and fosters a just and prosperous society.

8.2 Final Thoughts on Sovereign AI and National Advancement

Interplay Between Philosophy, AI, and Progress

As we stand on the precipice of unprecedented technological advancement, the integration of philosophy into the development and governance of artificial intelligence becomes not just beneficial, but essential. Philosophical grounding provides a moral compass that guides AI innovation, ensuring that technological progress does not outpace our ethical considerations. Without this foundation, we risk creating systems that, while efficient and intelligent, may lack the nuanced understanding of human values and societal norms that are crucial for harmonious coexistence.

Philosophy encourages us to ask the right questions: What constitutes fairness in AI decision-making? How do we balance efficiency with compassion? These inquiries are vital as we design AI systems that impact every facet of our lives. By embedding philosophical principles into AI development, we can create technologies that not only drive progress but also enhance human flourishing. AI has the potential to alleviate suffering, expand access to knowledge, and empower individuals in ways previously unimaginable. When aligned with our deepest ethical values, AI becomes a tool for profound good, fostering a society where technology serves humanity's highest aspirations.

Future Beyond the AI Revolution

Looking beyond the current AI revolution, the future holds a landscape of continuous evolution and boundless pursuit of knowledge. As AI systems become more sophisticated, we may venture into realms where artificial general intelligence (AGI) and quantum computing redefine our understanding of intelligence and computation. These advancements promise to unlock solutions to some of humanity's most intractable problems, from climate change to healthcare disparities, propelling us into a new era of innovation and discovery.

However, this journey requires us to remain vigilant and adaptable. The relentless pace of technological change demands a commitment to lifelong learning and an openness to new ideas. As we navigate this future, the pursuit of knowledge must be tempered with wisdom, ensuring that each step forward is measured and mindful of its broader implications. Sovereign AI will continue to evolve, necessitating dynamic governance structures and ethical frameworks that can keep pace with innovation.

Ultimately, the future beyond the AI revolution is not a destination but an ongoing voyage. It is a testament to humanity's enduring quest to understand, shape, and improve the world around us. By maintaining a steadfast commitment to philosophical inquiry and ethical stewardship, we can ensure that each wave of technological advancement contributes to a more just, equitable, and enlightened society. Sovereign AI, therefore, is not just about harnessing technology—it is about shaping a future where AI and humanity thrive together, united by shared values and a common vision for progress.

References

1. Turing, A. M. (1950). Computing Machinery and Intelligence. Mind, 59(236), 433–460.
2. Wiener, N. (1950). The Human Use of Human Beings: Cybernetics and Society. Houghton Mifflin.
3. Asimov, I. (1950). I, Robot. Gnome Press.
4. Bostrom, N. (2014). Superintelligence: Paths, Dangers, Strategies. Oxford University Press.
5. Kurzweil, R. (2005). The Singularity Is Near: When Humans Transcend Biology. Viking Press.
6. Habermas, J. (1984). The Theory of Communicative Action. Beacon Press.
7. Buolamwini, J., & Gebru, T. (2018). Gender Shades: Intersectional Accuracy Disparities in Commercial Gender Classification. Proceedings of Machine Learning Research, 81, 1–15.
8. Kant, I. (1795). Perpetual Peace: A Philosophical Sketch.
9. Anderson, B. (1983). Imagined Communities: Reflections on the Origin and Spread of Nationalism. Verso.
10. Dewey, J. (1938). Experience and Education. Macmillan.
11. Mill, J. S. (1859). On Liberty. John W. Parker and Son.
12. Nagel, T. (1974). What Is It Like to Be a Bat? The Philosophical Review, 83(4), 435–450.
13. Bentham, J. (1789). An Introduction to the Principles of Morals and Legislation.
14. Kant, I. (1785). Groundwork of the Metaphysics of Morals.
15. Aristotle. (4th century BCE). Nicomachean Ethics.
16. Singer, P. W. (2009). Wired for War: The Robotics Revolution and Conflict in the 21st Century.
17. Scharre, P. (2018). Army of None: Autonomous Weapons and the Future of War.
18. Government of India, NITI Aayog. (2018). National Strategy for Artificial Intelligence #AIForAll. Retrieved from https://niti.gov.in/national-strategy-artificial-intelligence
19. AgriLedger. (2021). Empowering Farmers with Blockchain and AI. Retrieved from https://www.agriledger.io/
20. Cabinet Office, Government of Japan. (2017). Artificial Intelligence Technology Strategy. Retrieved from https://www8.cao.go.jp/cstp/english/humancentricai.pdf